Printed in the United States of America

# Link coloring

https://www.instagram.com/linkcoloring/

https://www.pinterest.com/linkcoloring/

https://twitter.com/Linkcoloring

Author : Link Coloring
Illustrated : Alexandra Ponomarenko

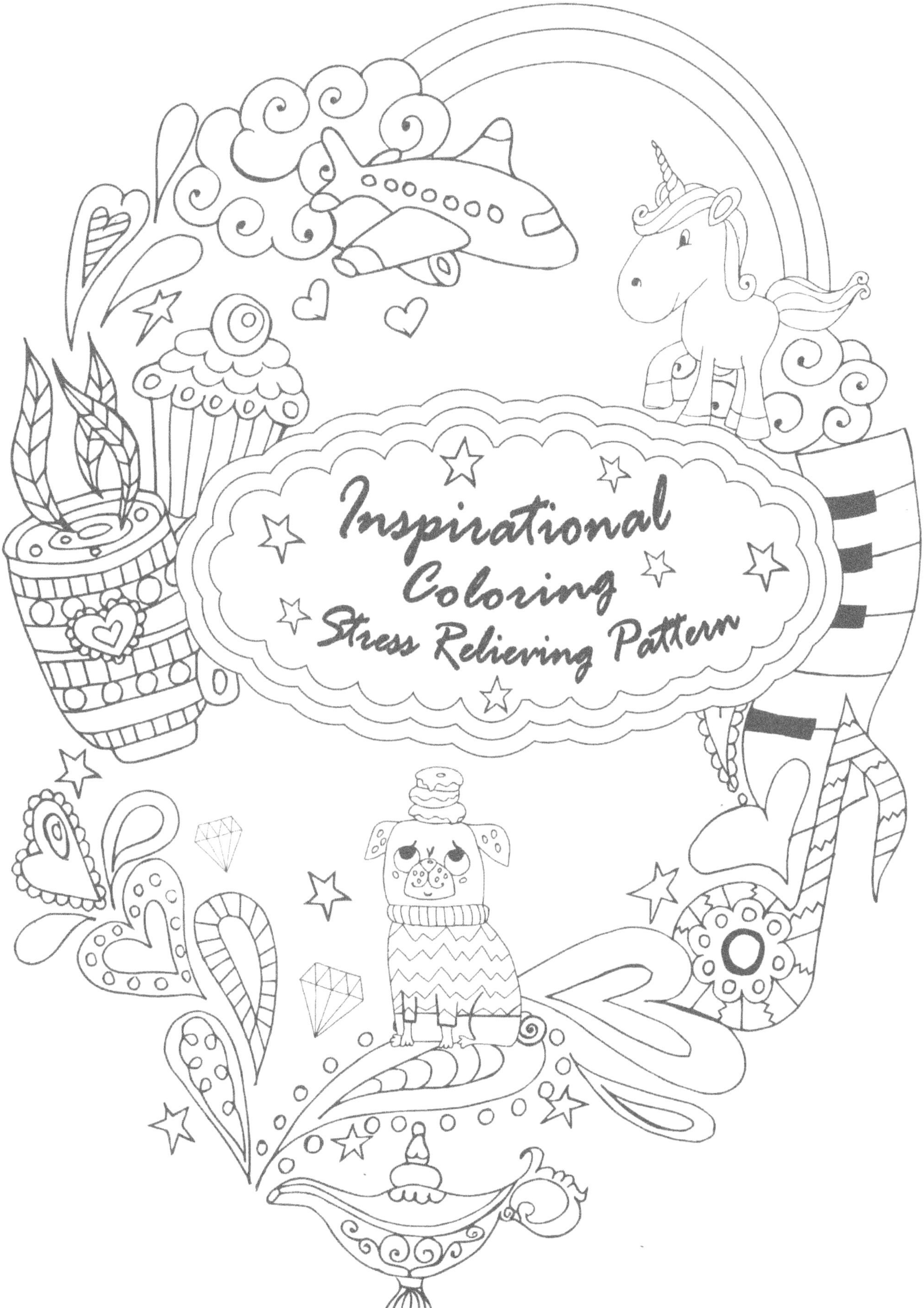
Inspirational
Coloring
Stress Relieving Pattern

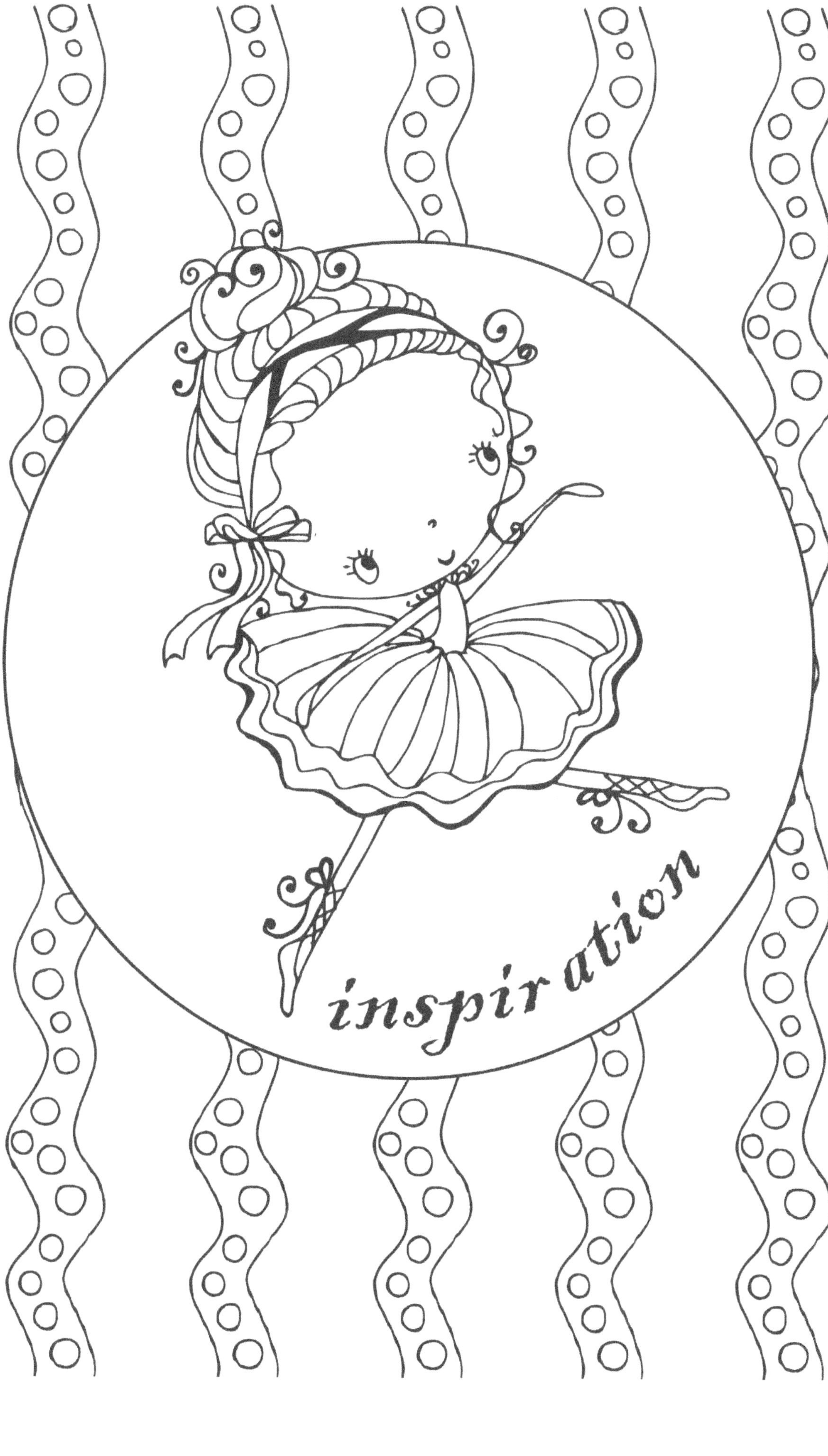
inspiration

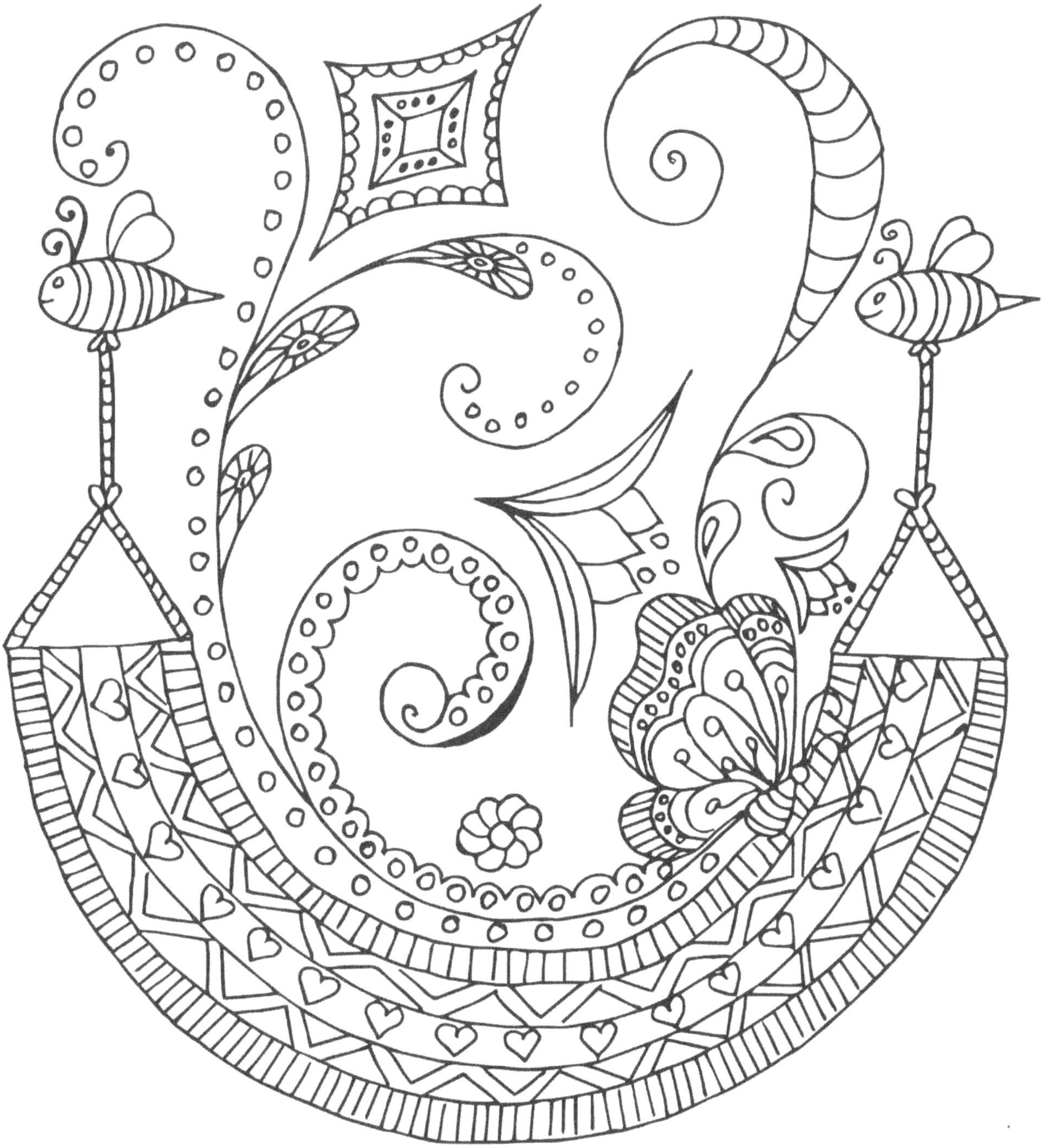

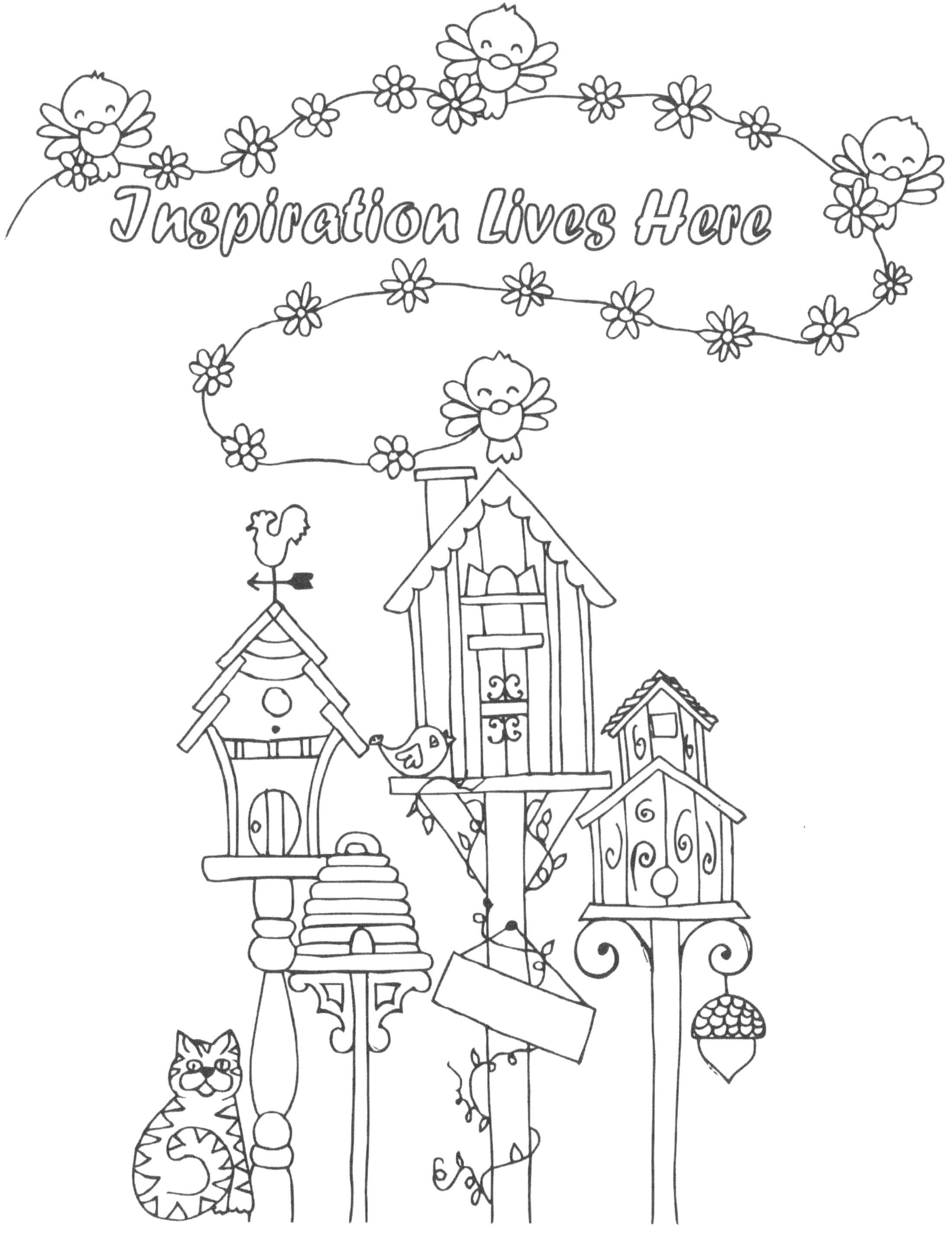
Inspiration Lives Here

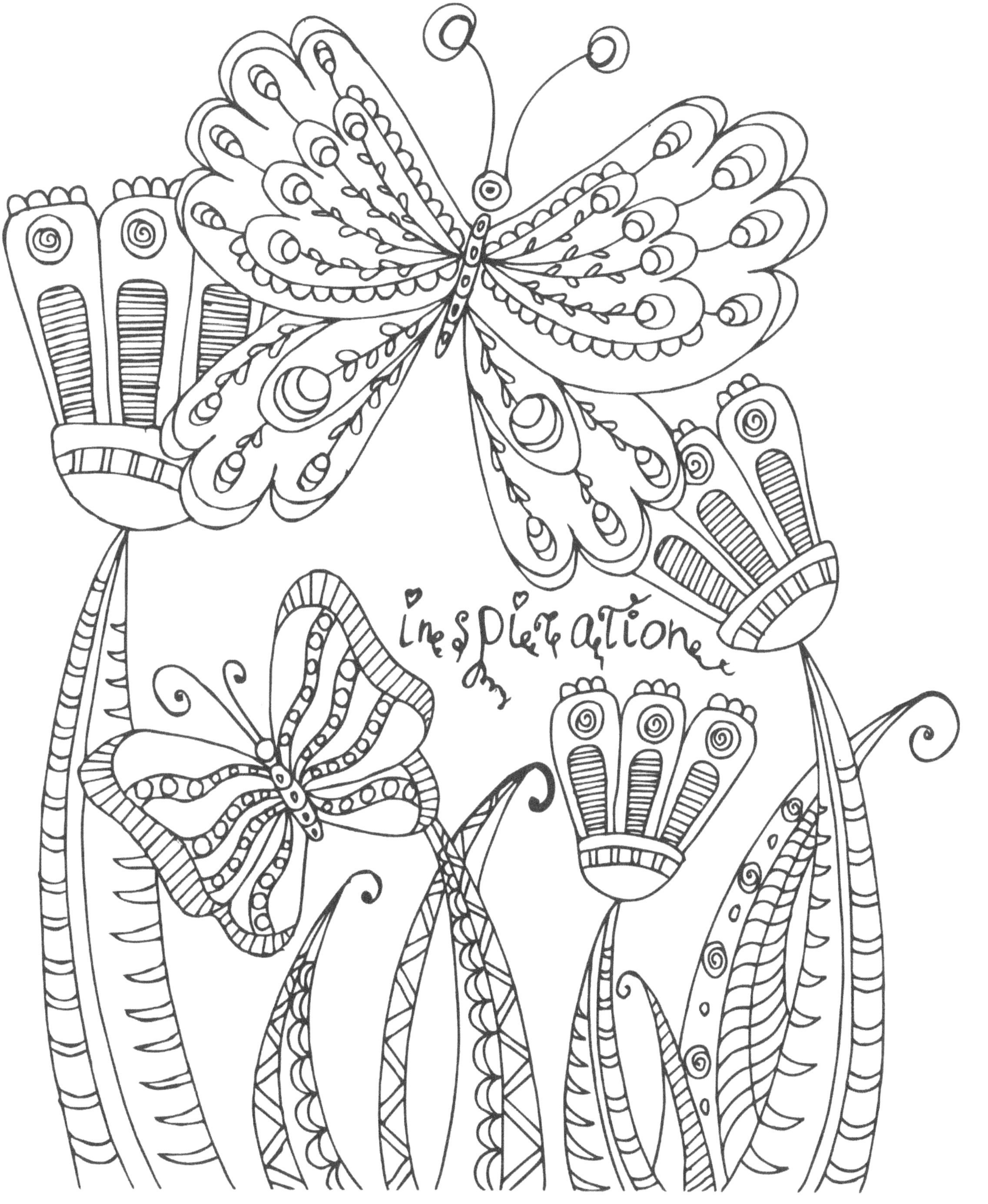
inspiration

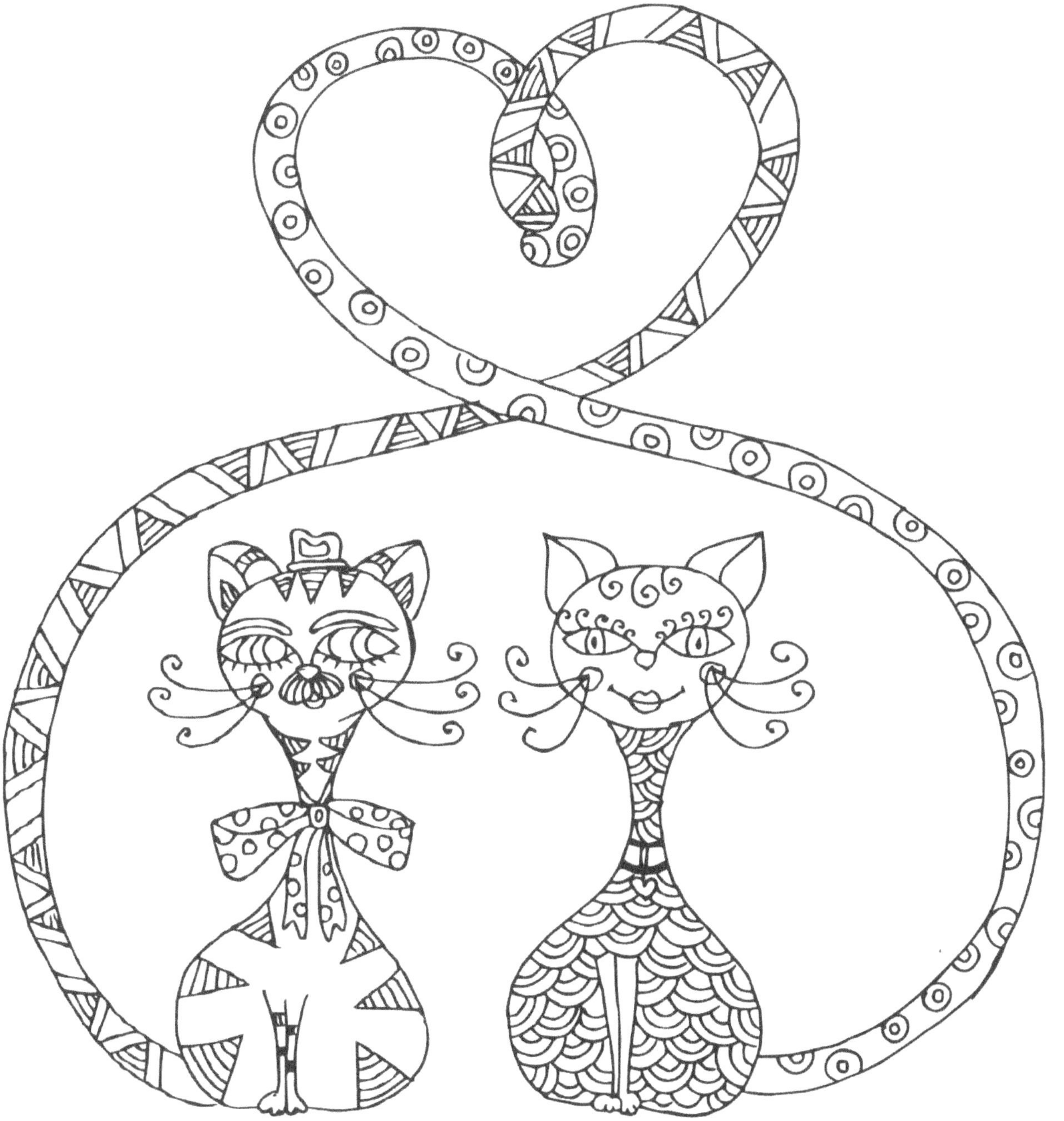

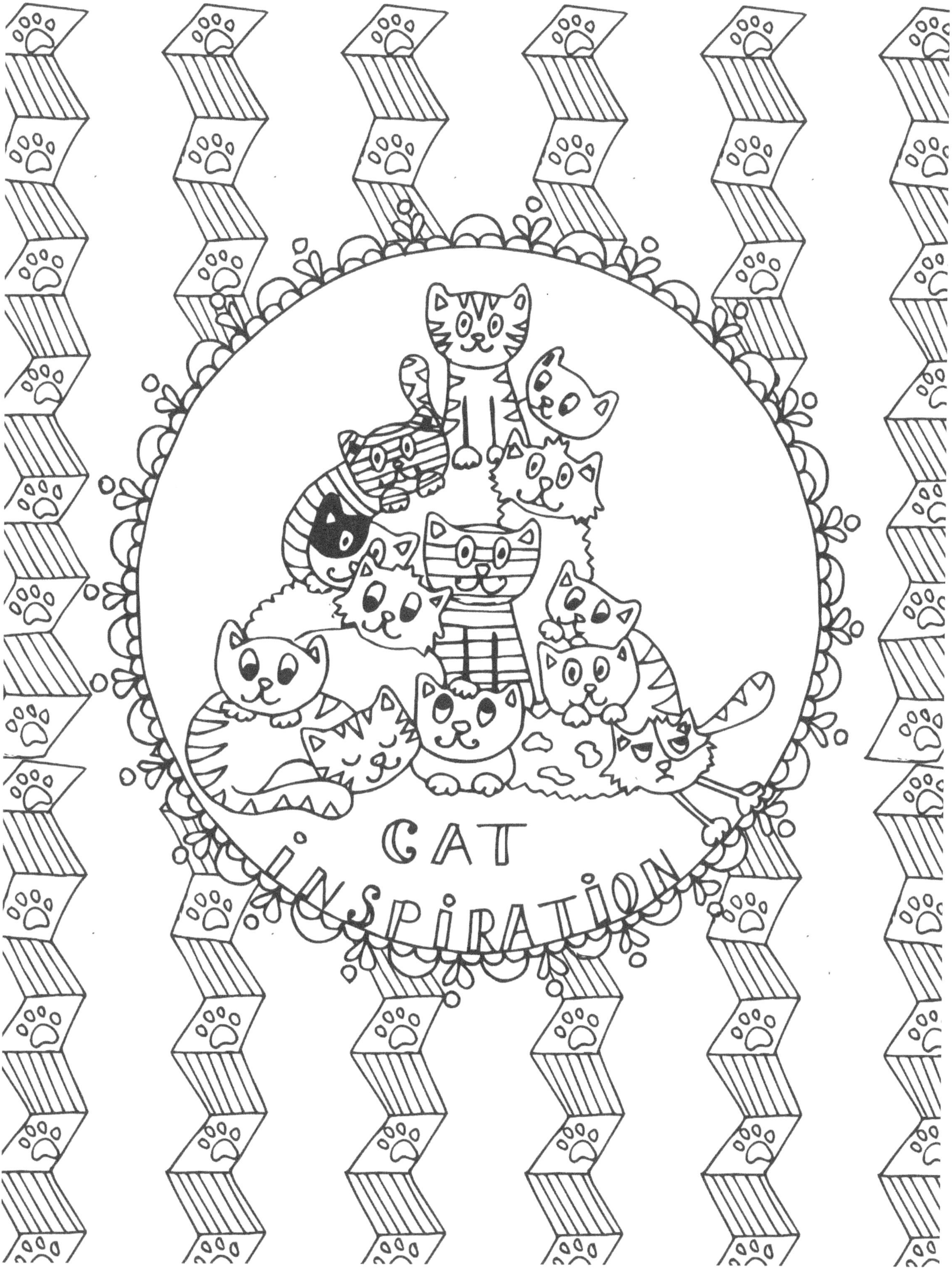
CAT
INSPIRATION

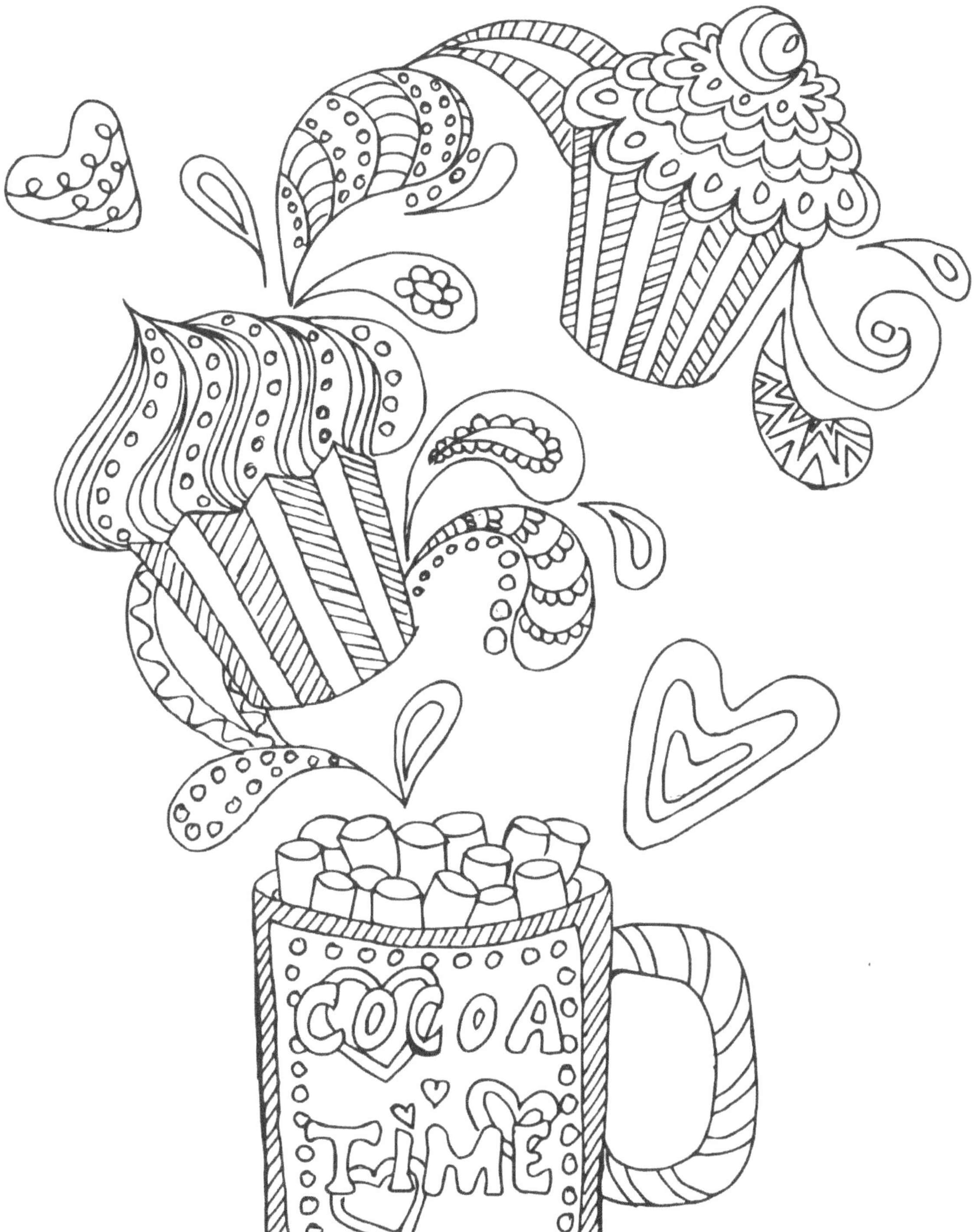
COCOA
TIME

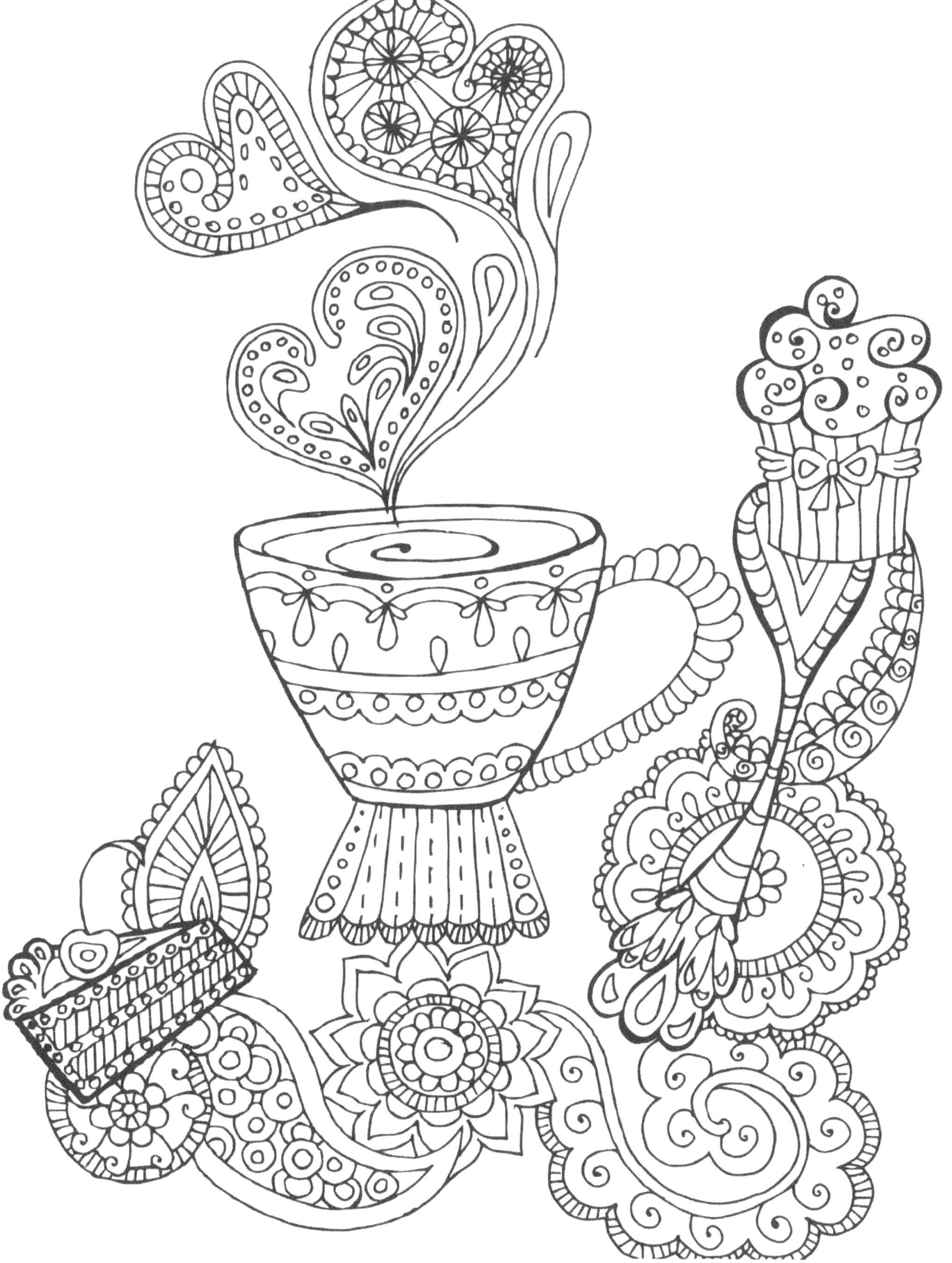

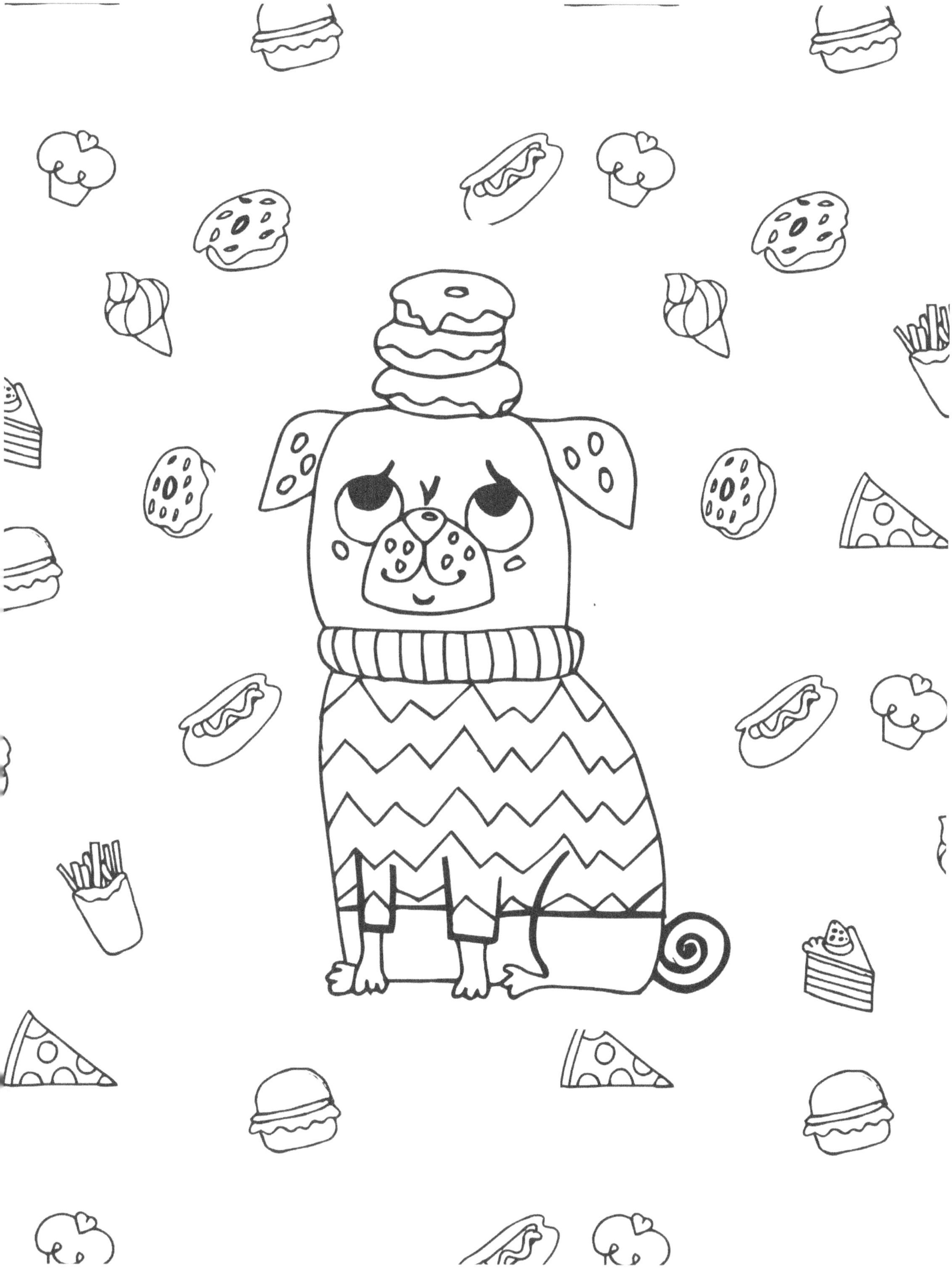

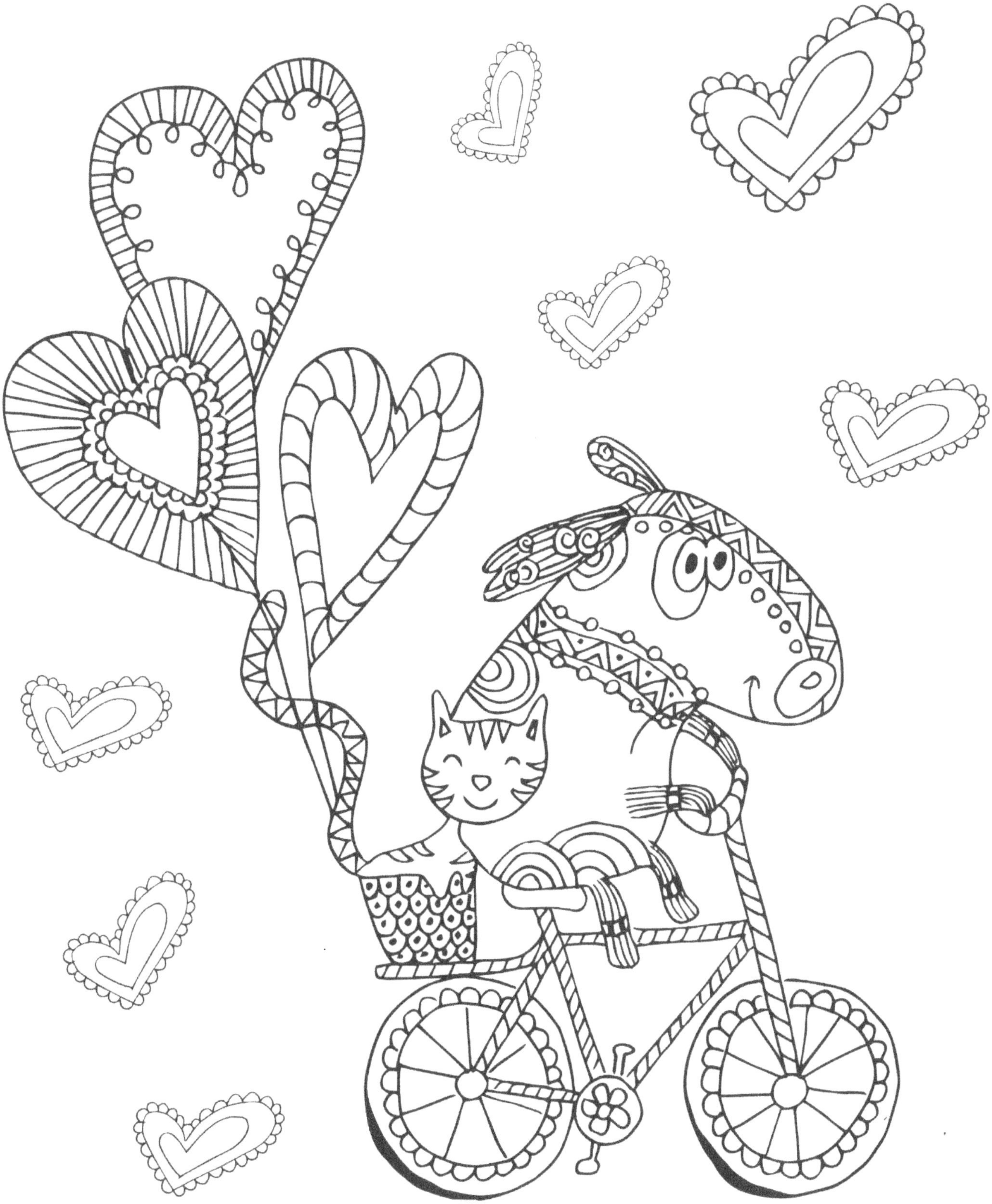

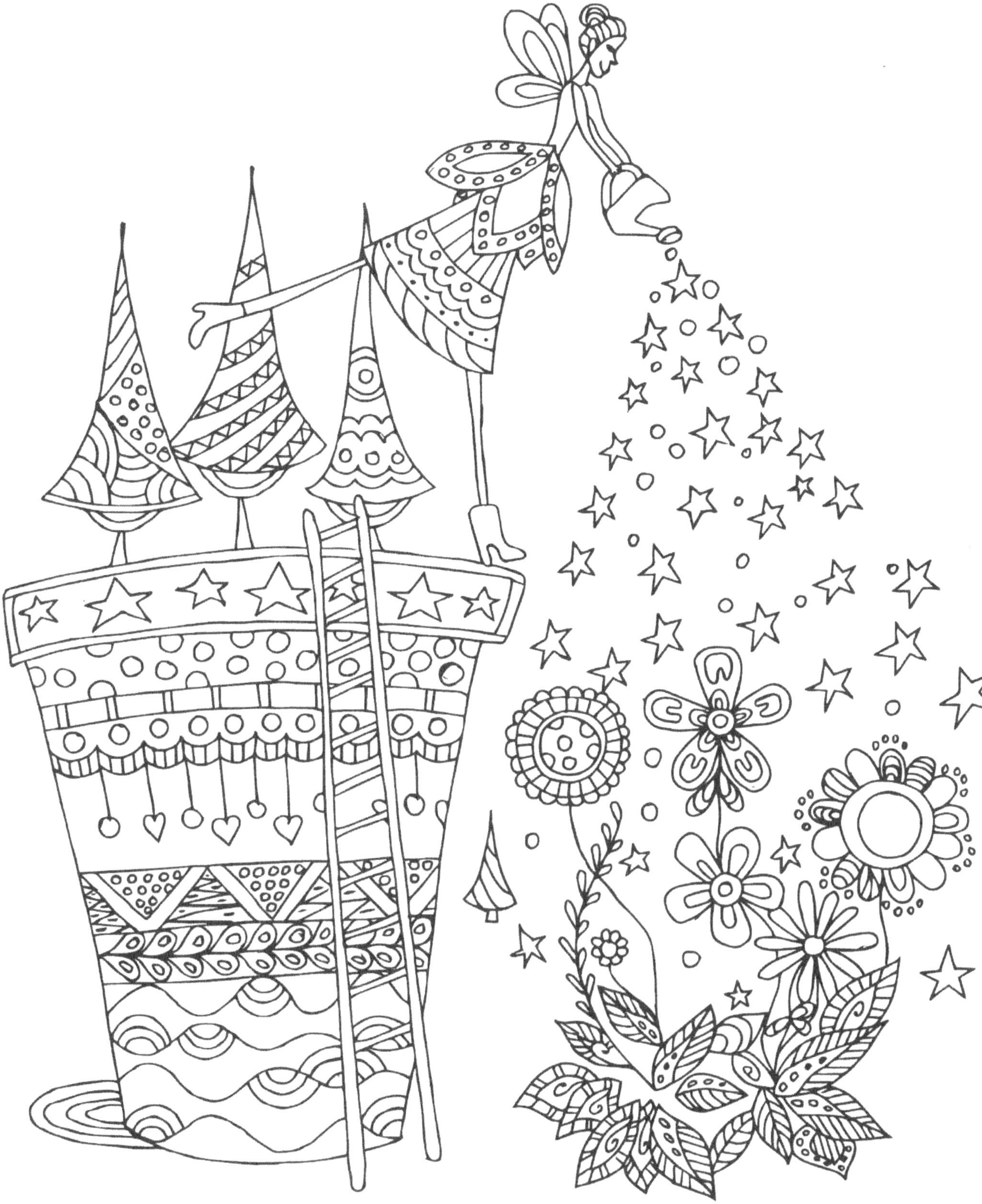

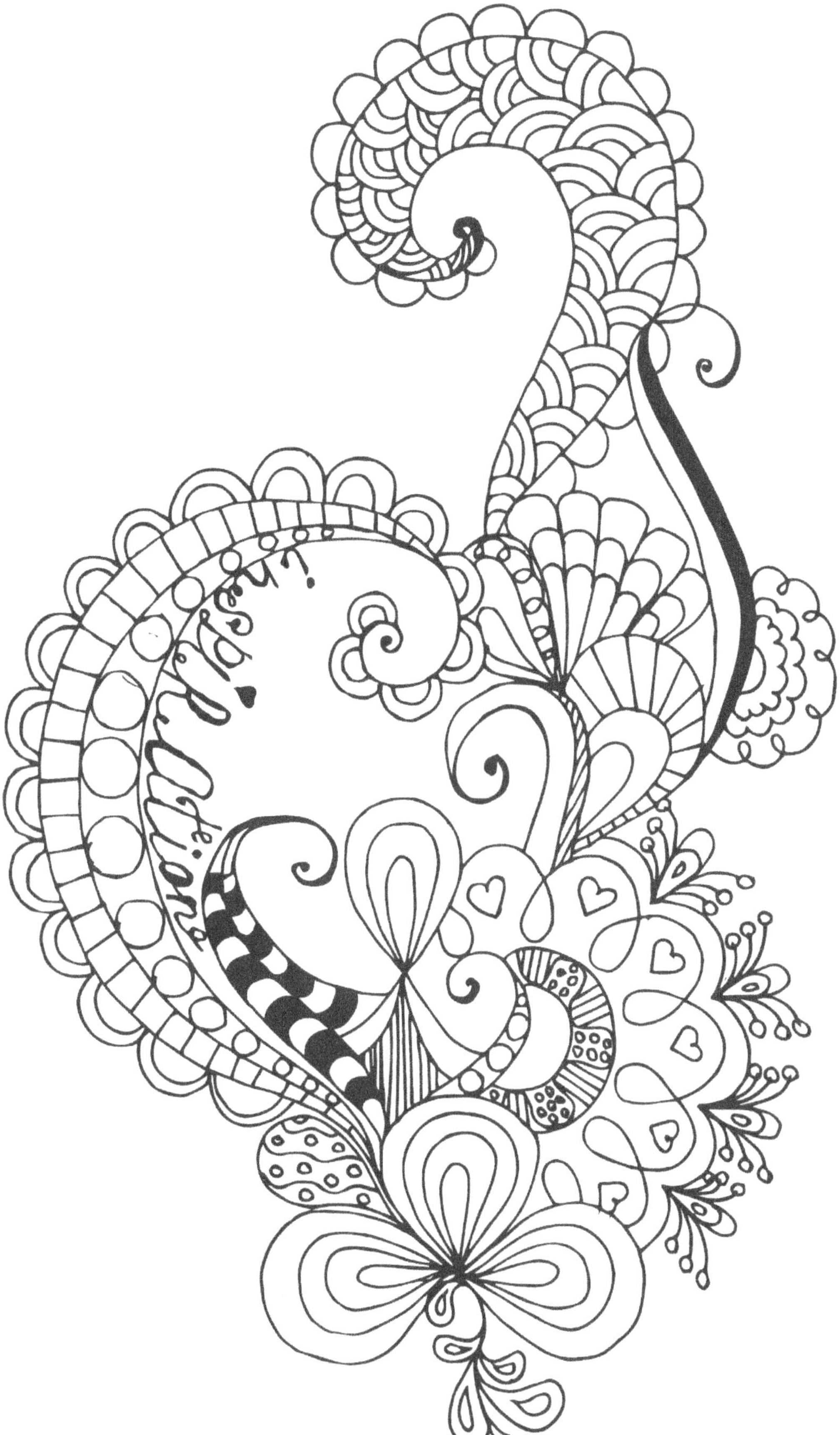
inspiration

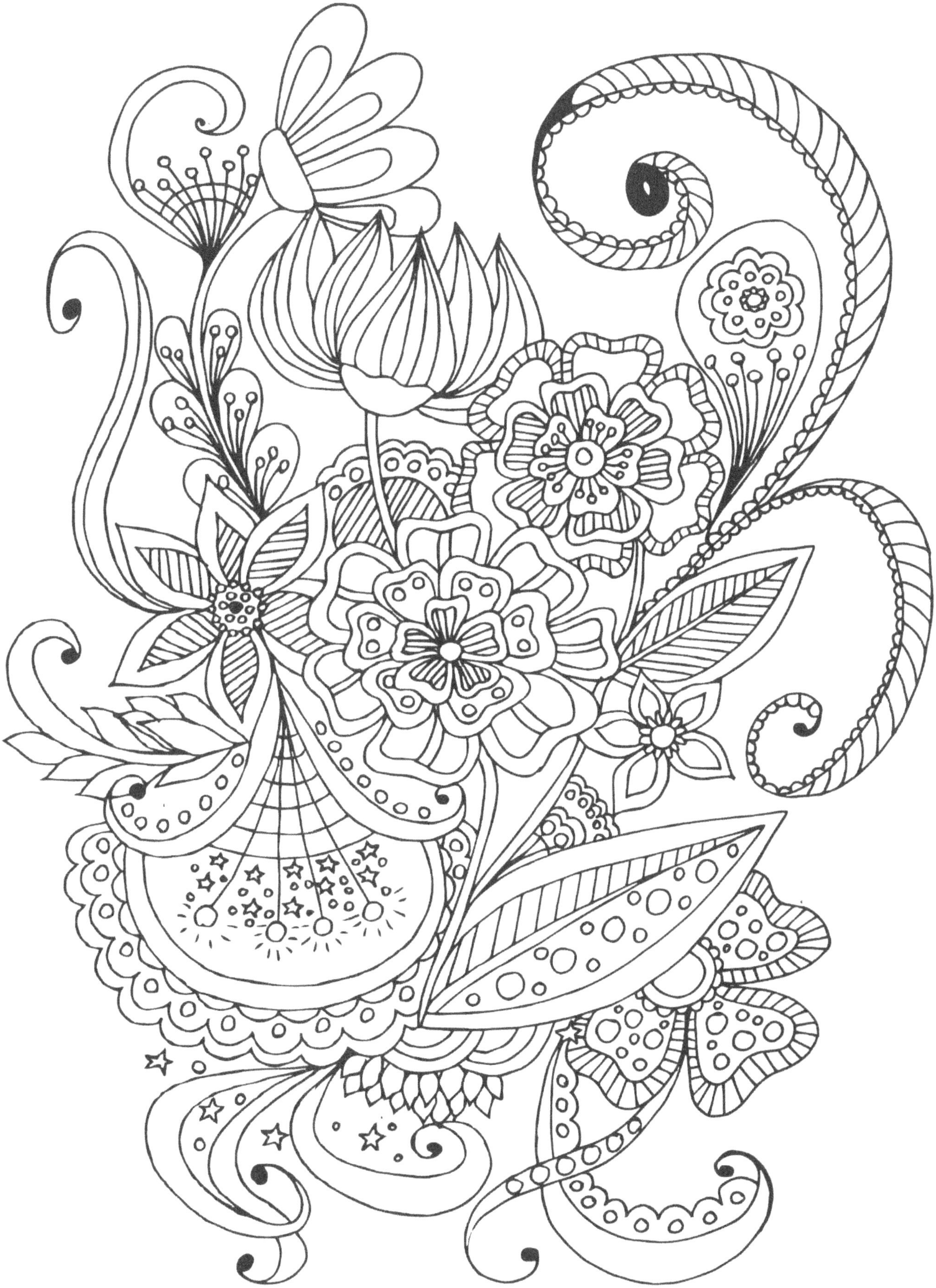

Where is your INSPIRATION

HIDDEN?

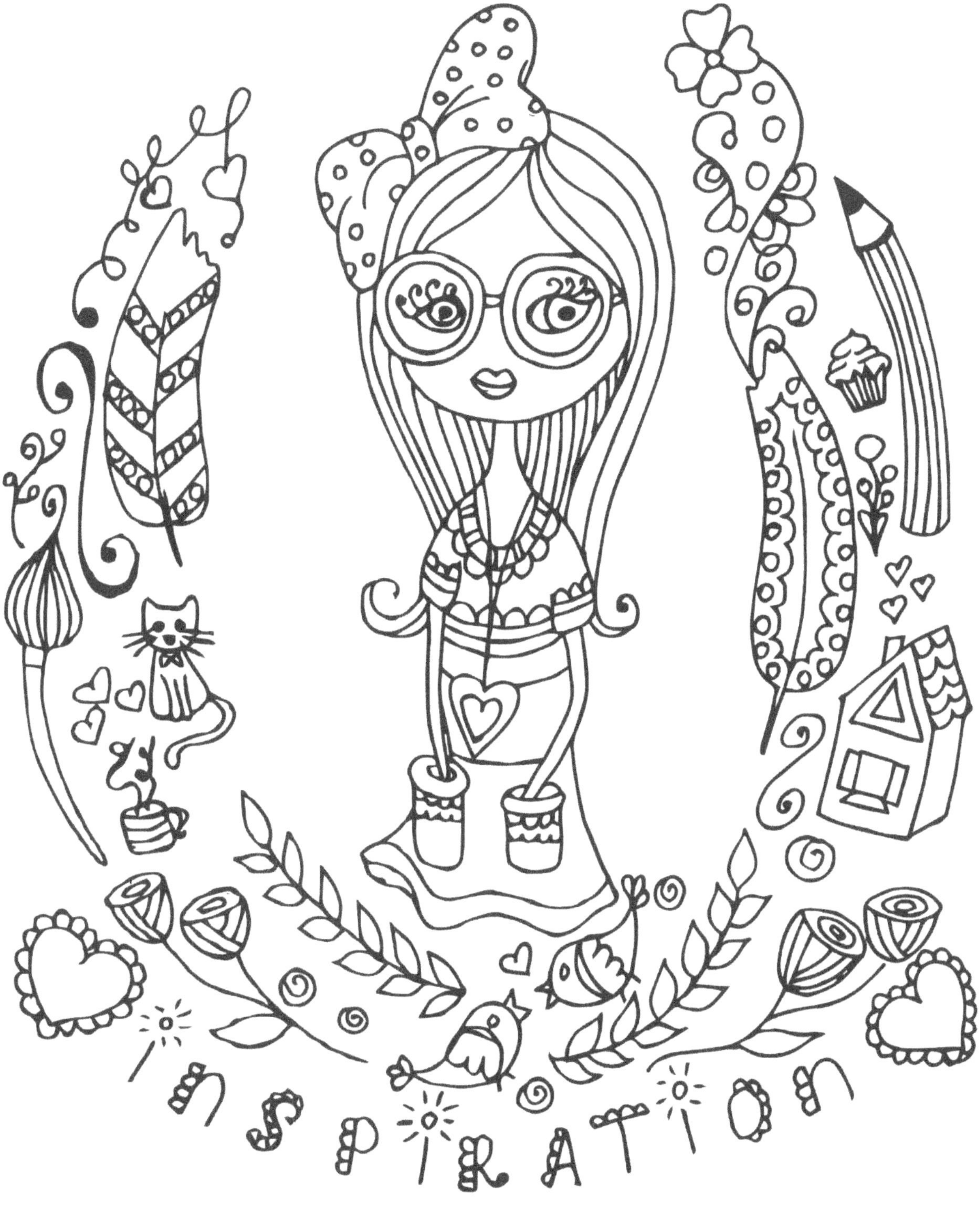
INSPIRATION

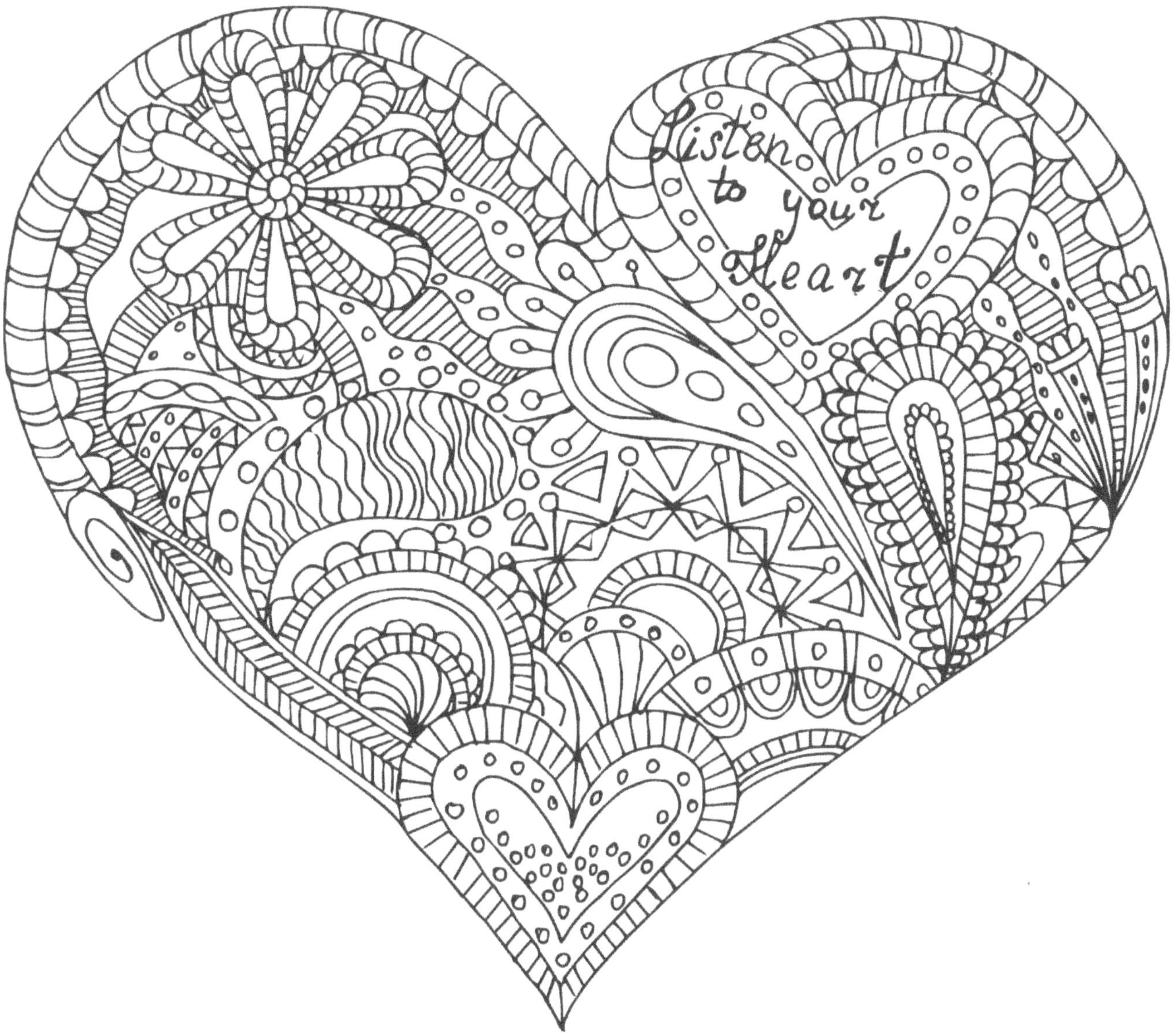
Listen
to your
Heart

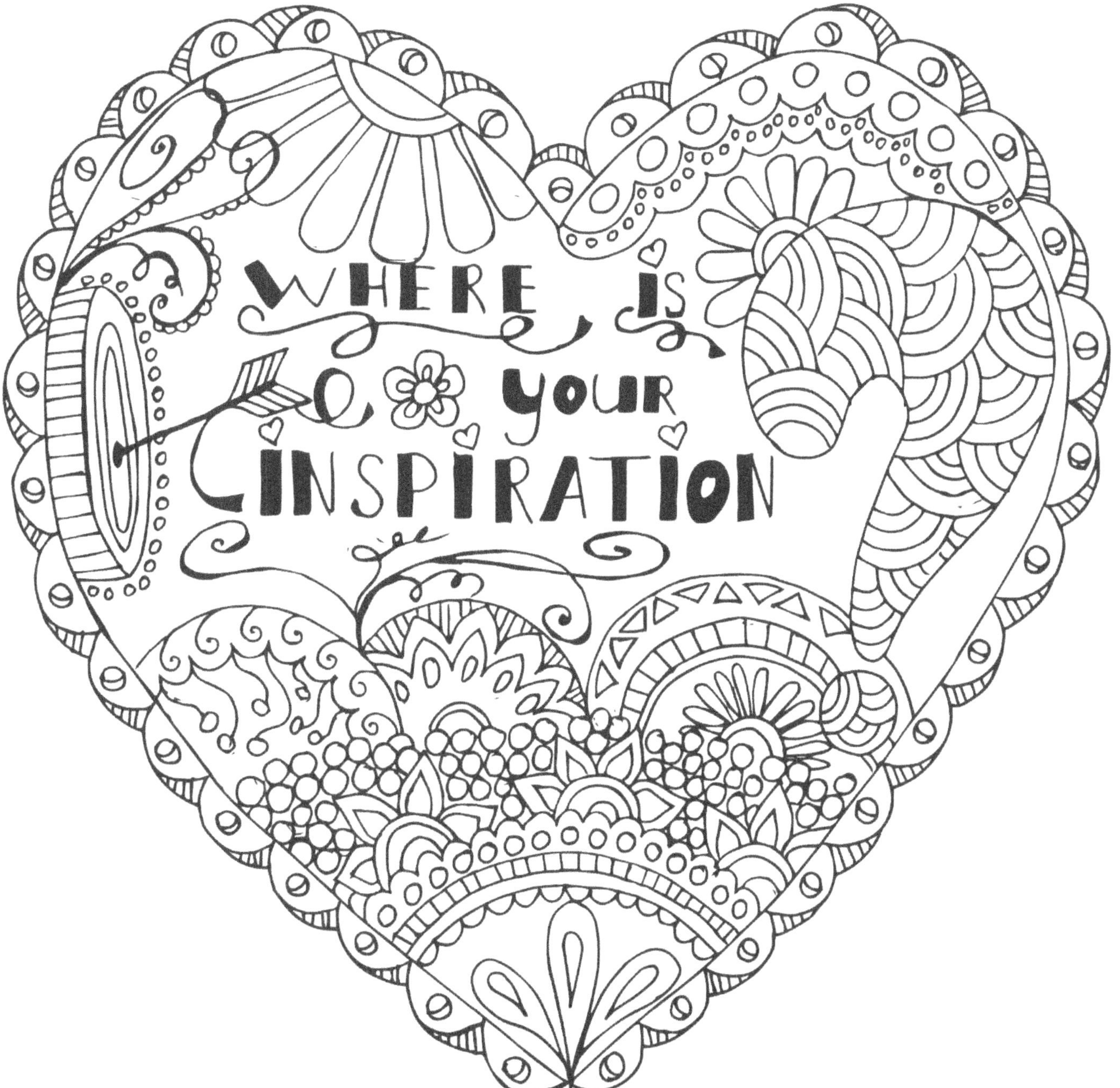
Where is
your
INSPIRATION

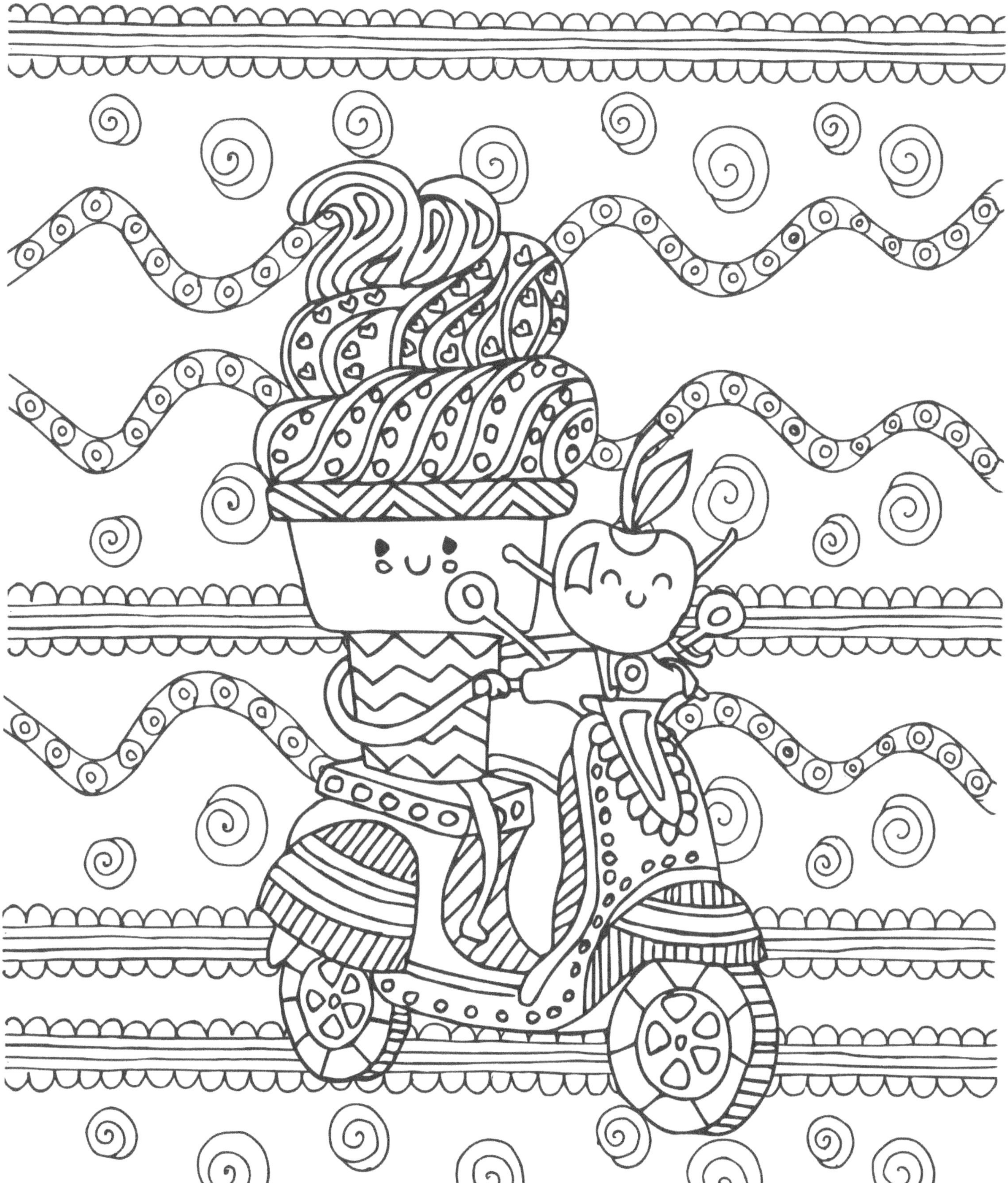

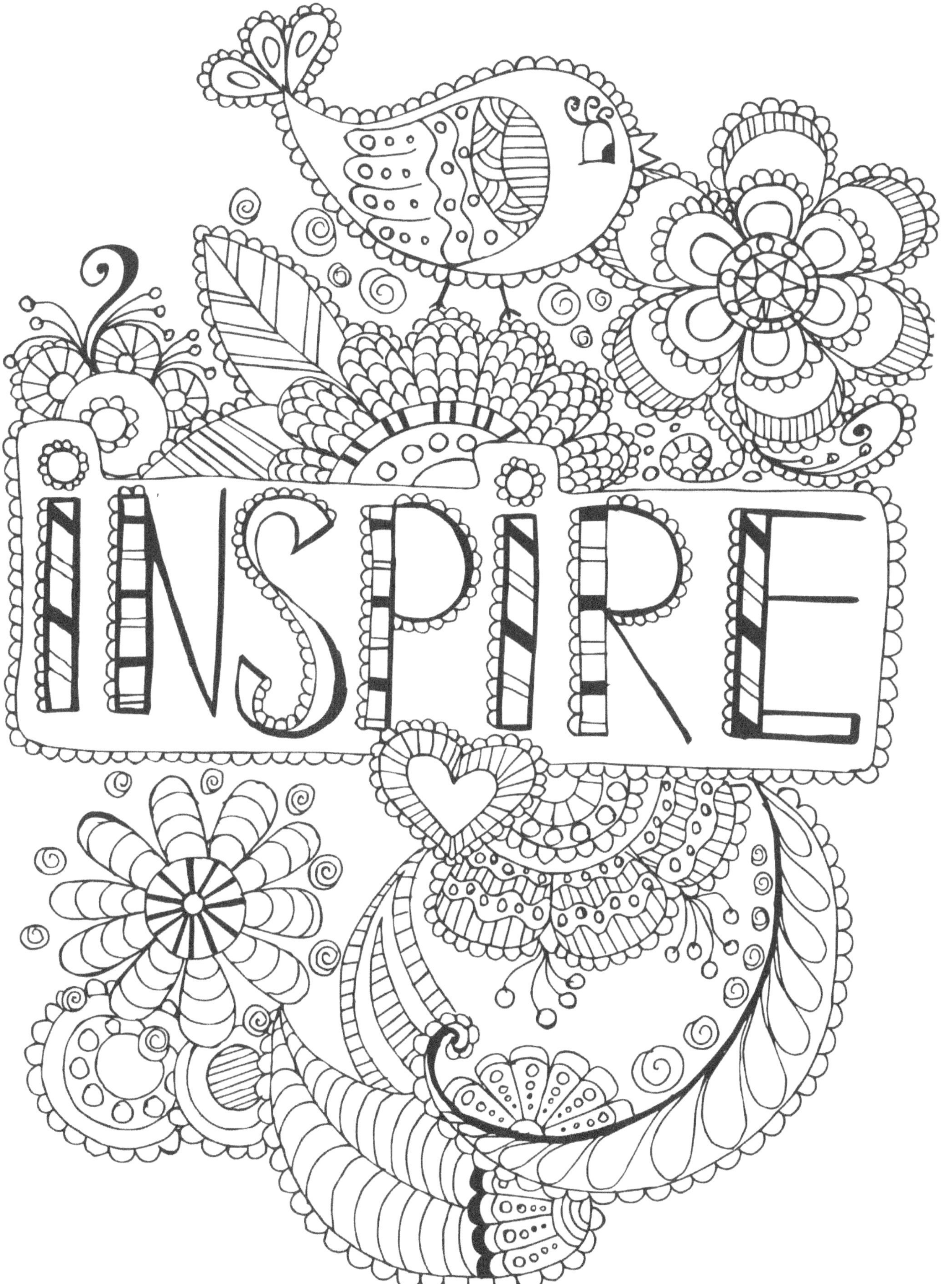
INSPIRE

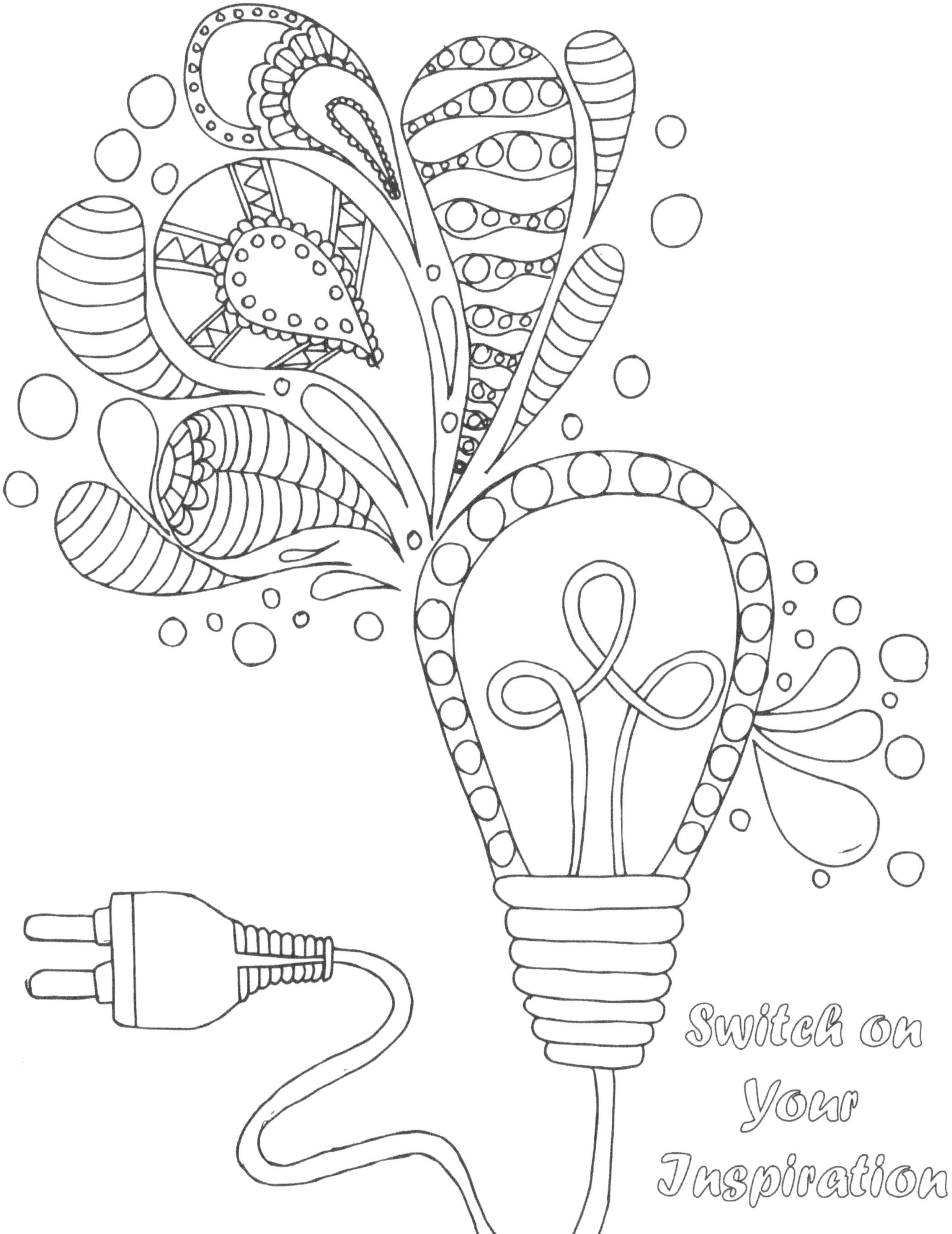
Switch on
Your
Inspiration

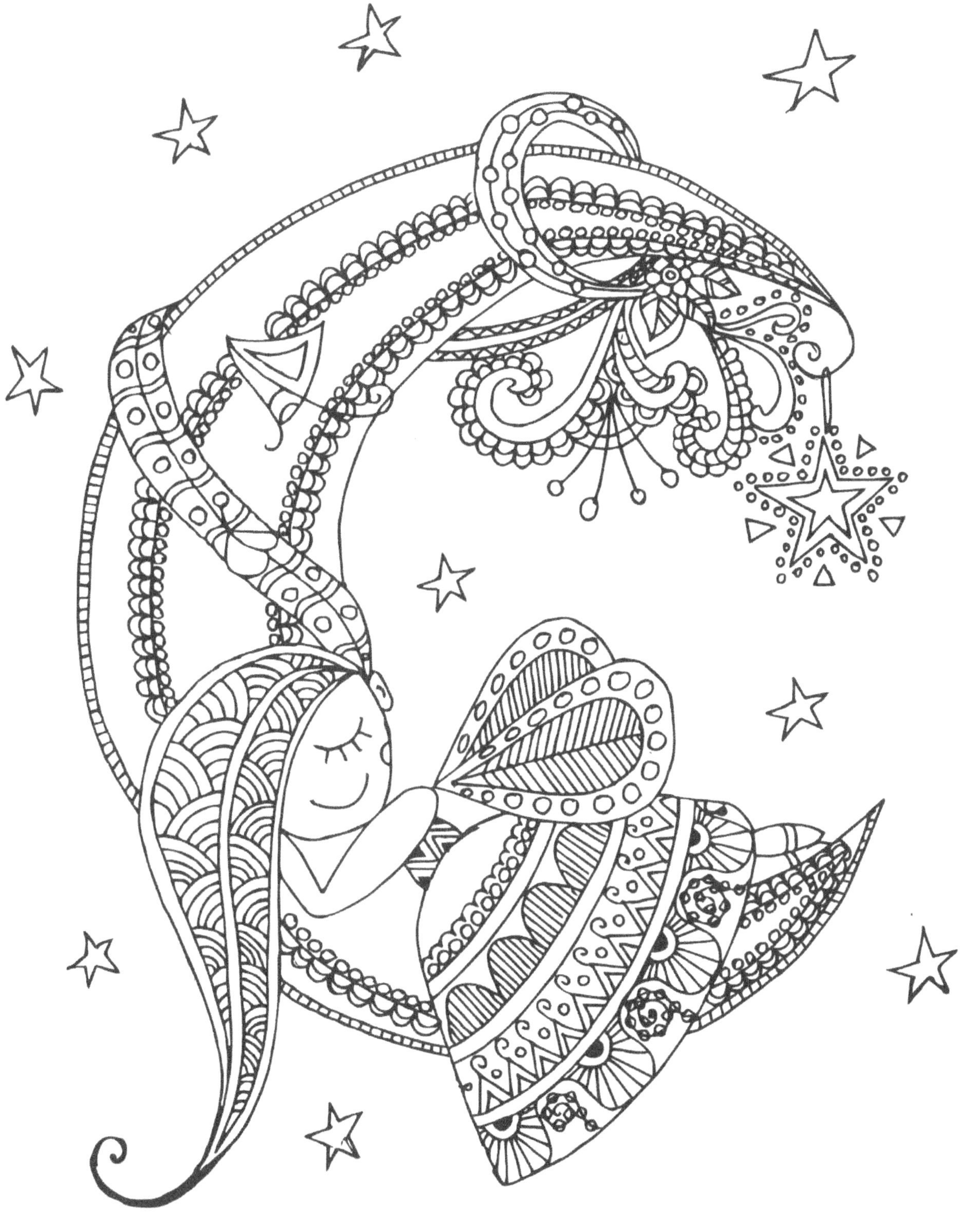

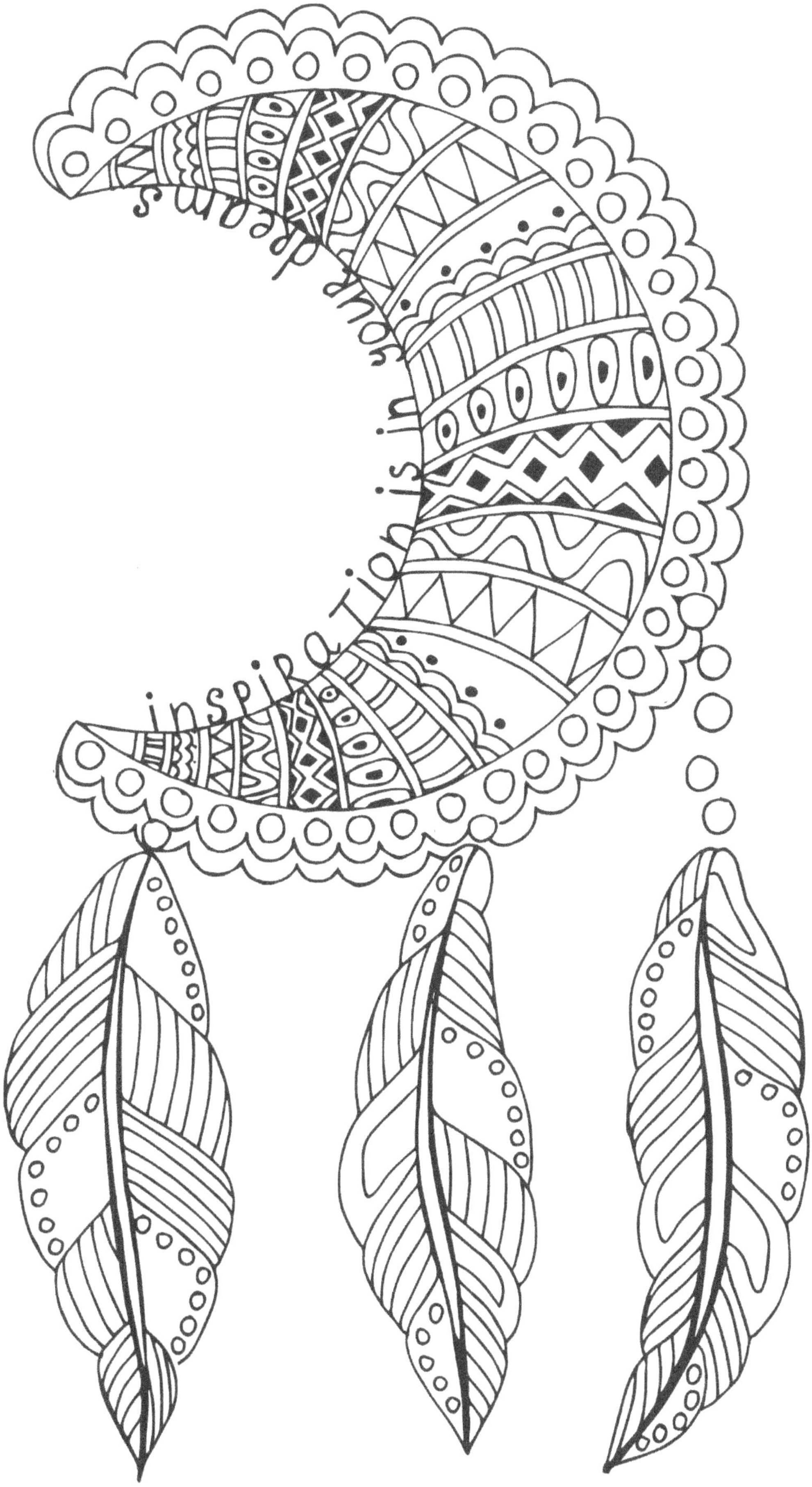
inspiration is in your dreams

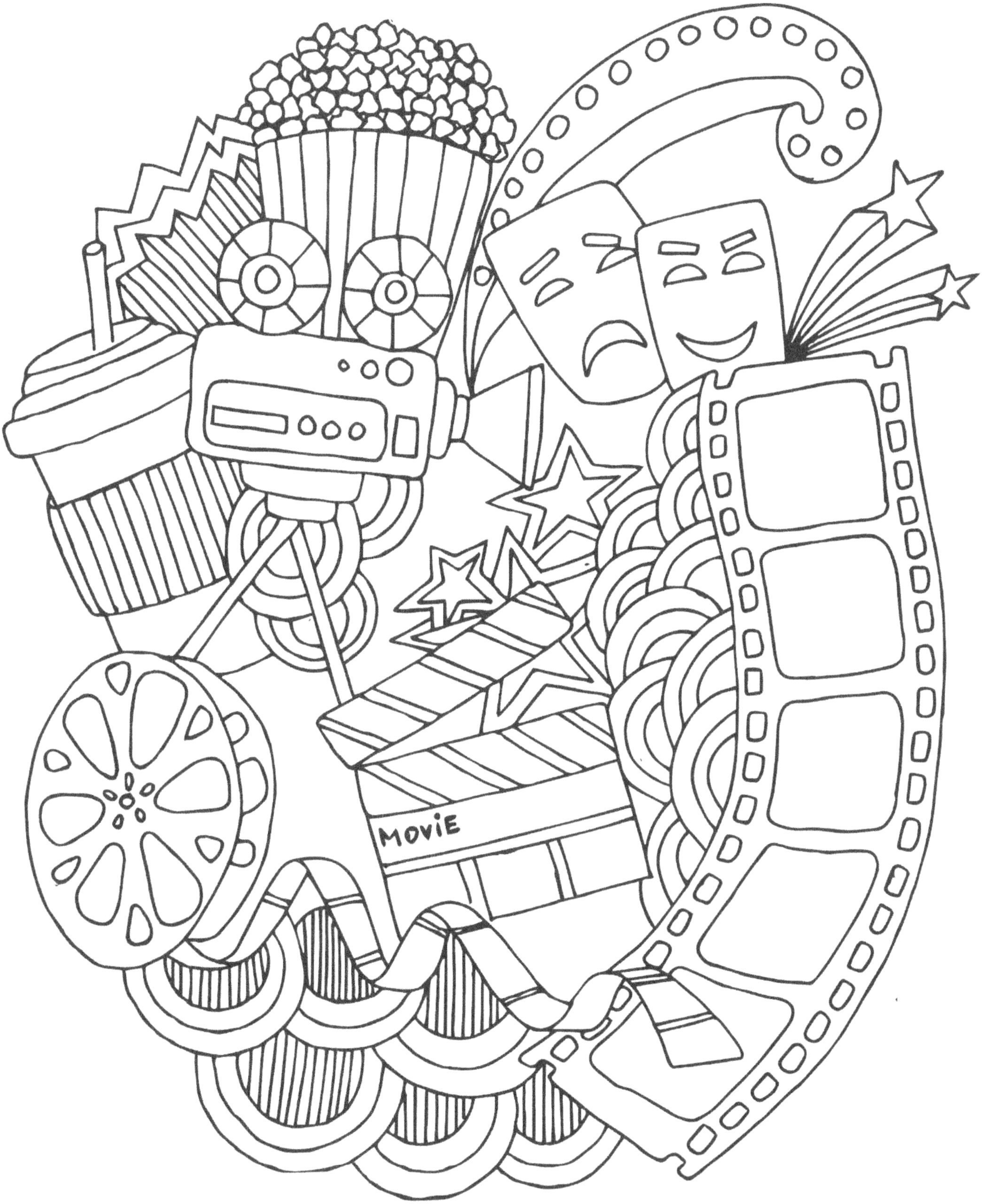
MOVIE

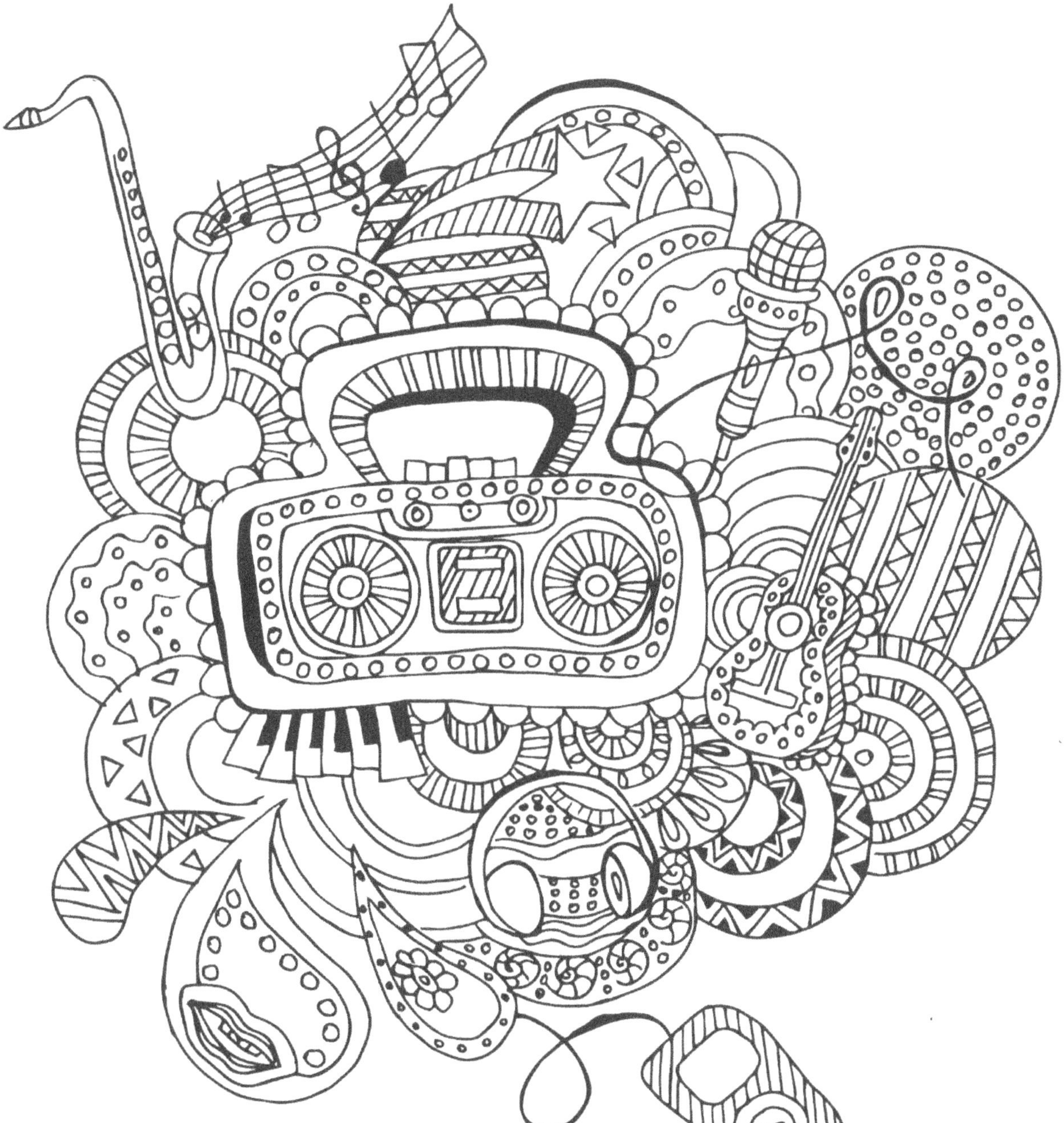

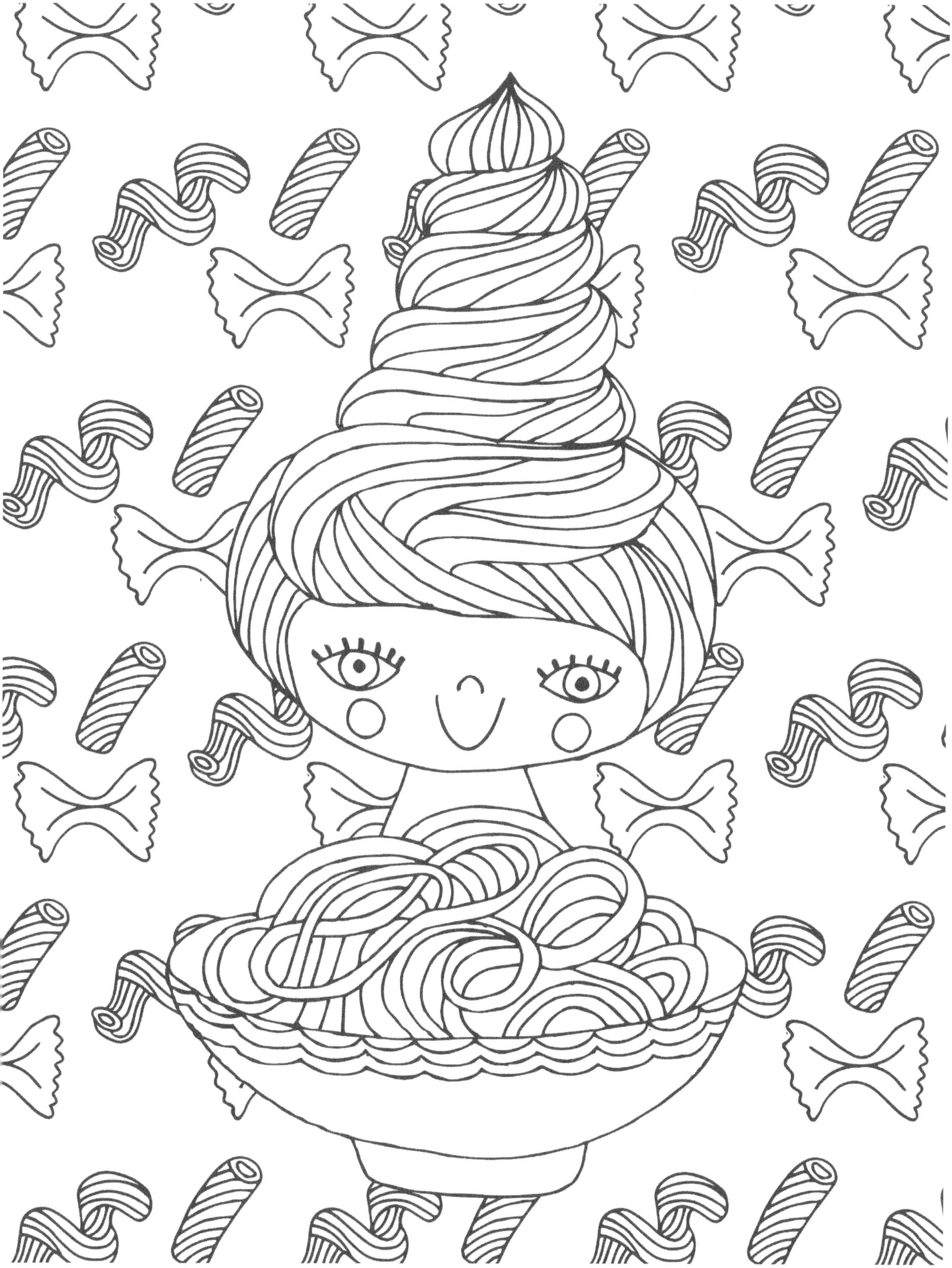

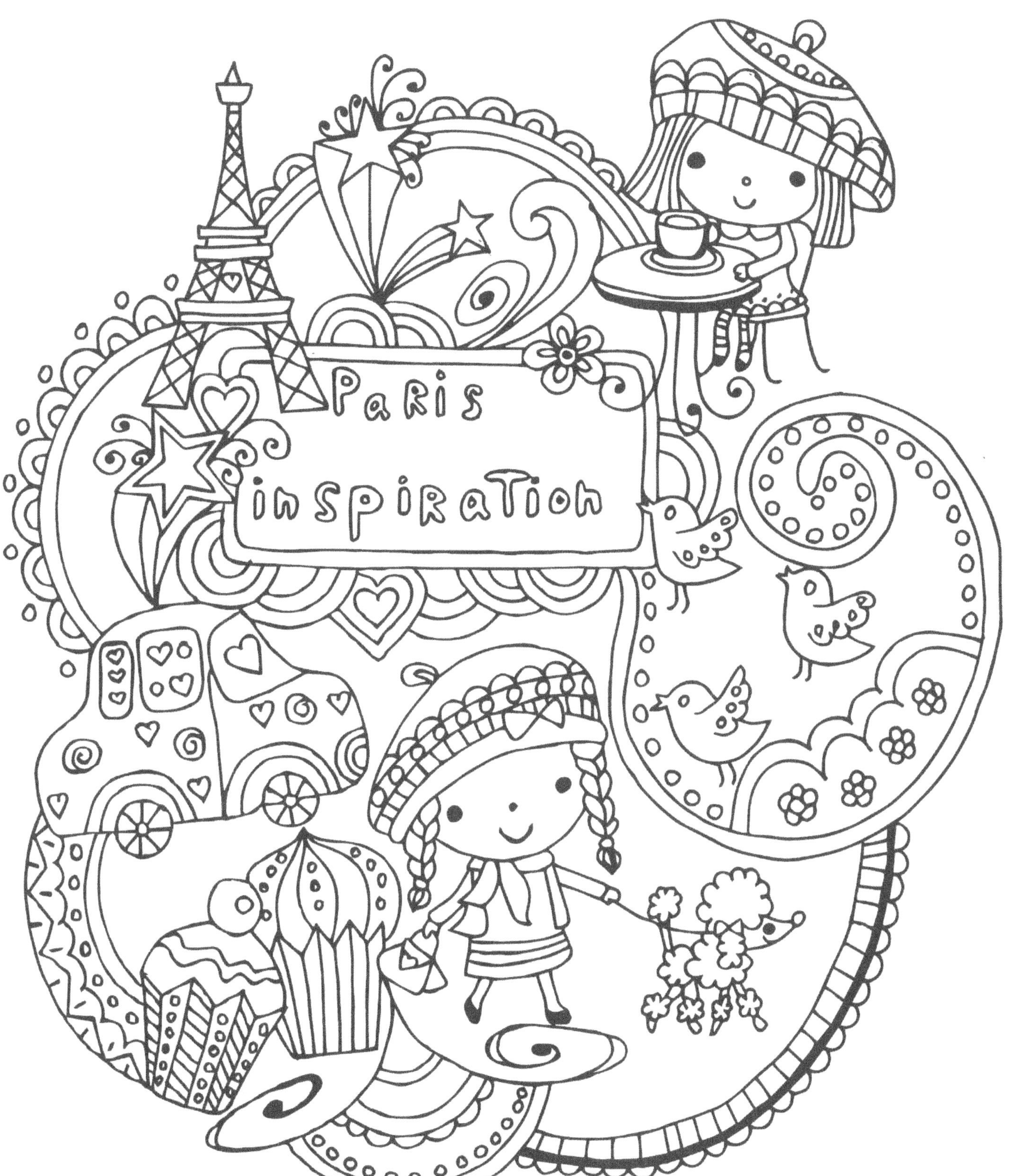
Paris
inspiration

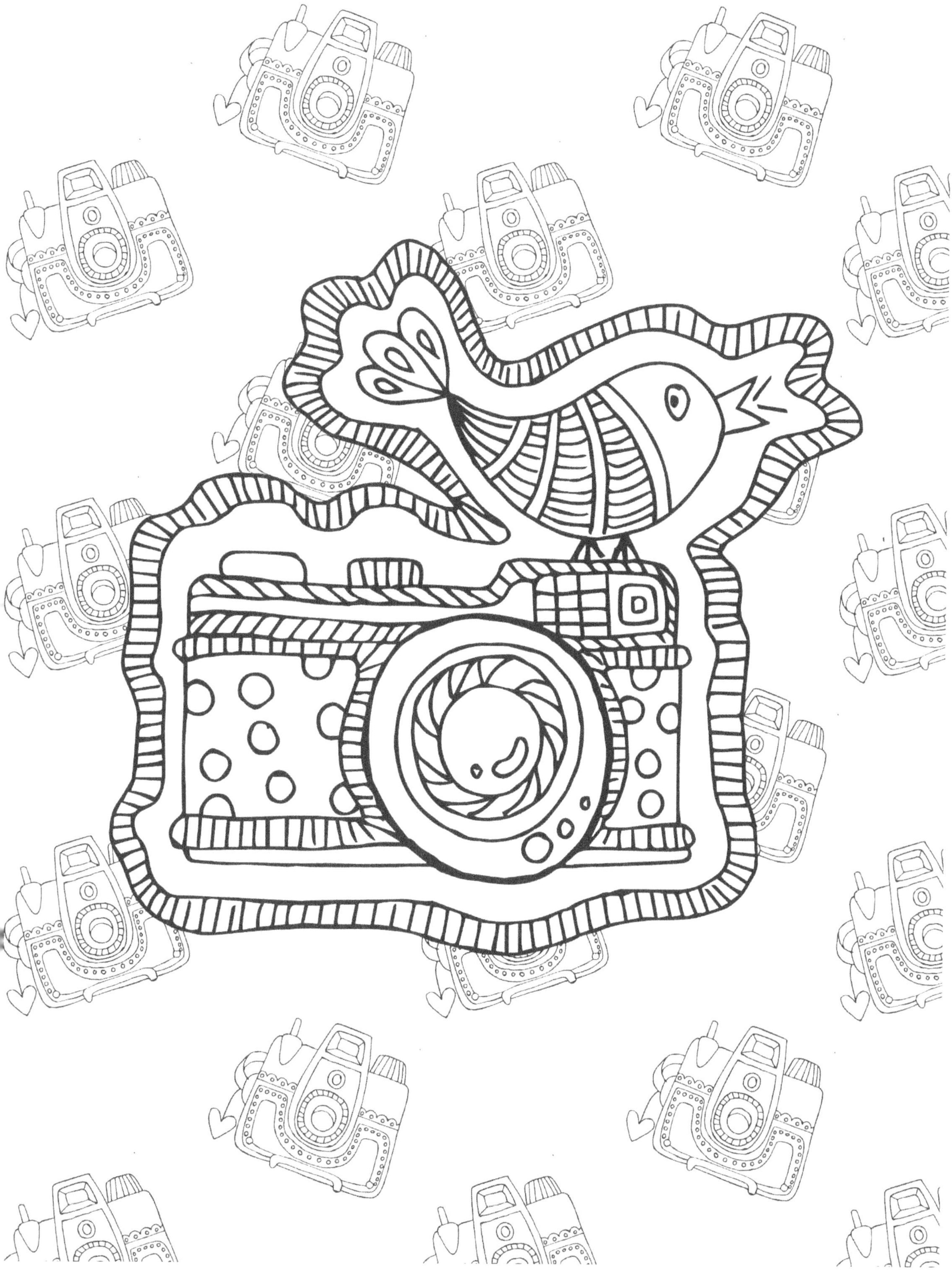

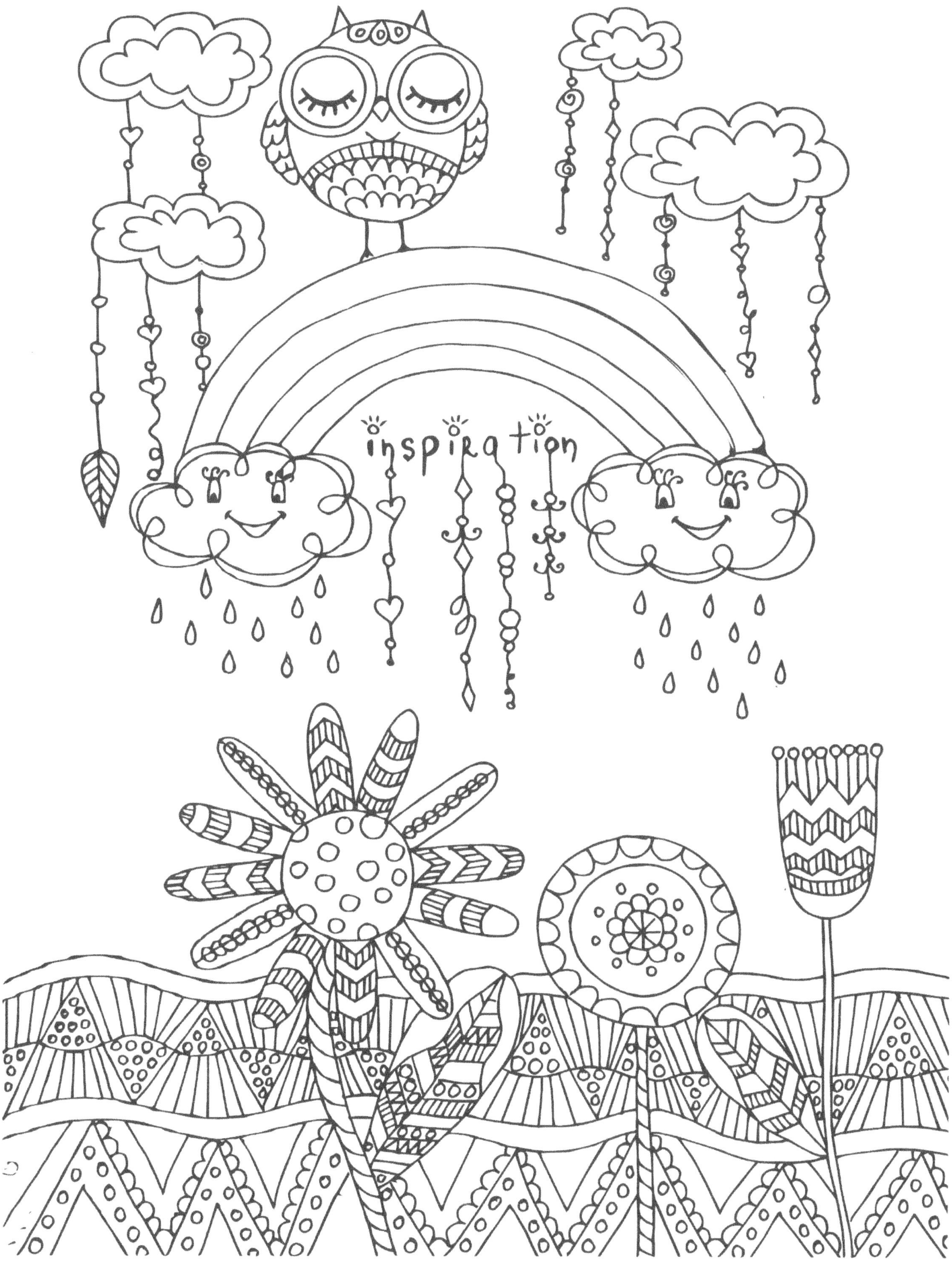
inspiration

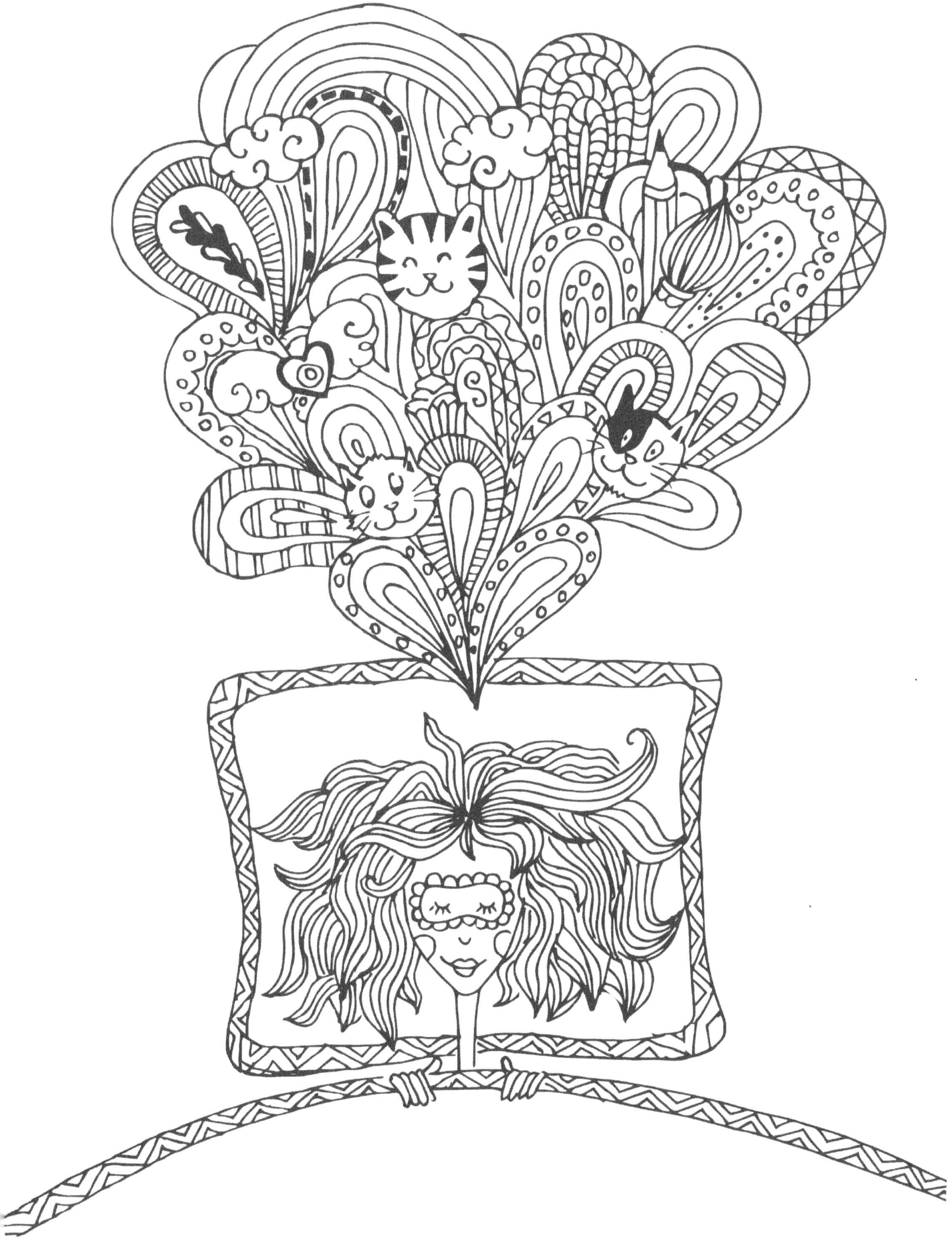

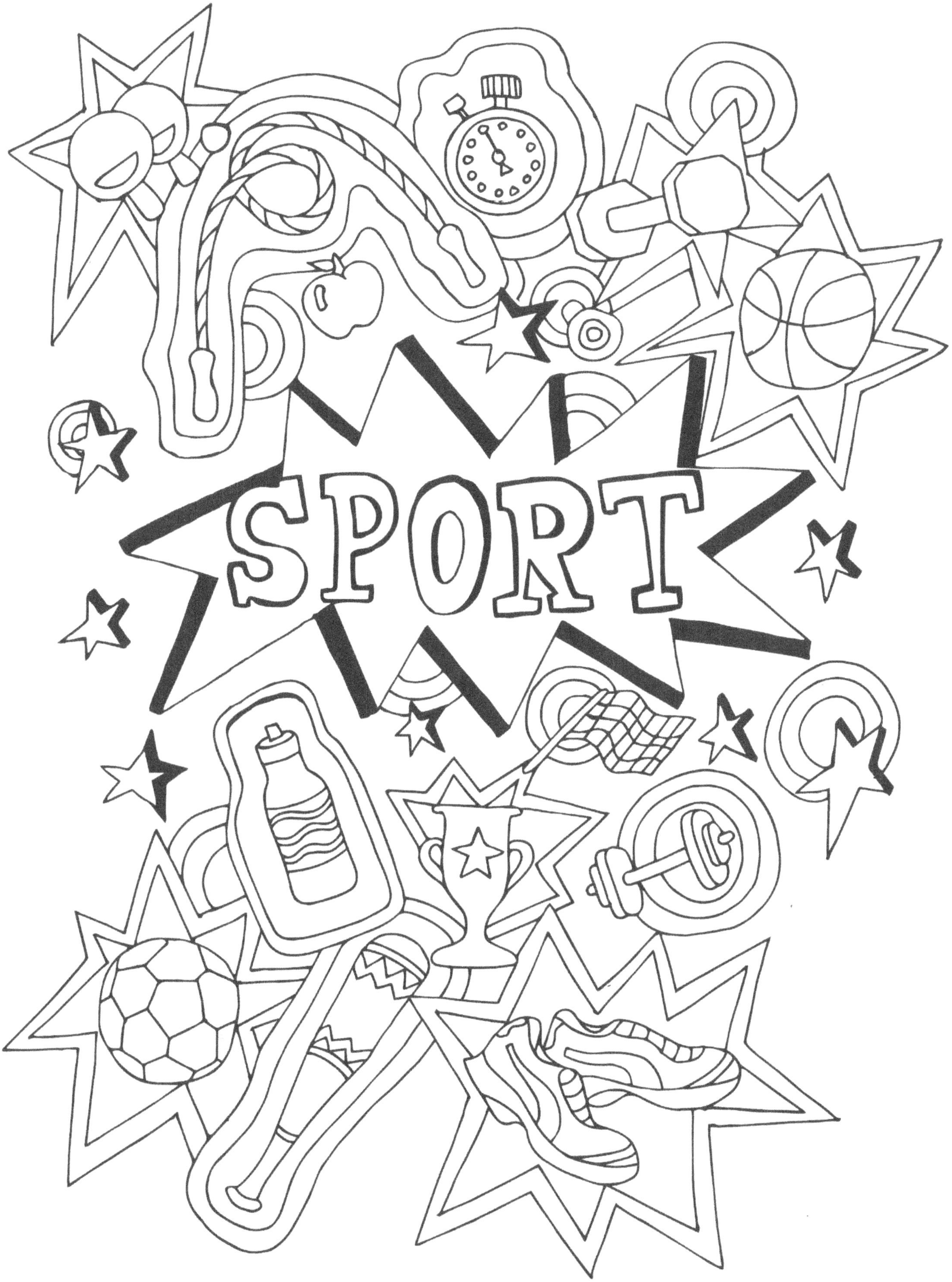
SPORT

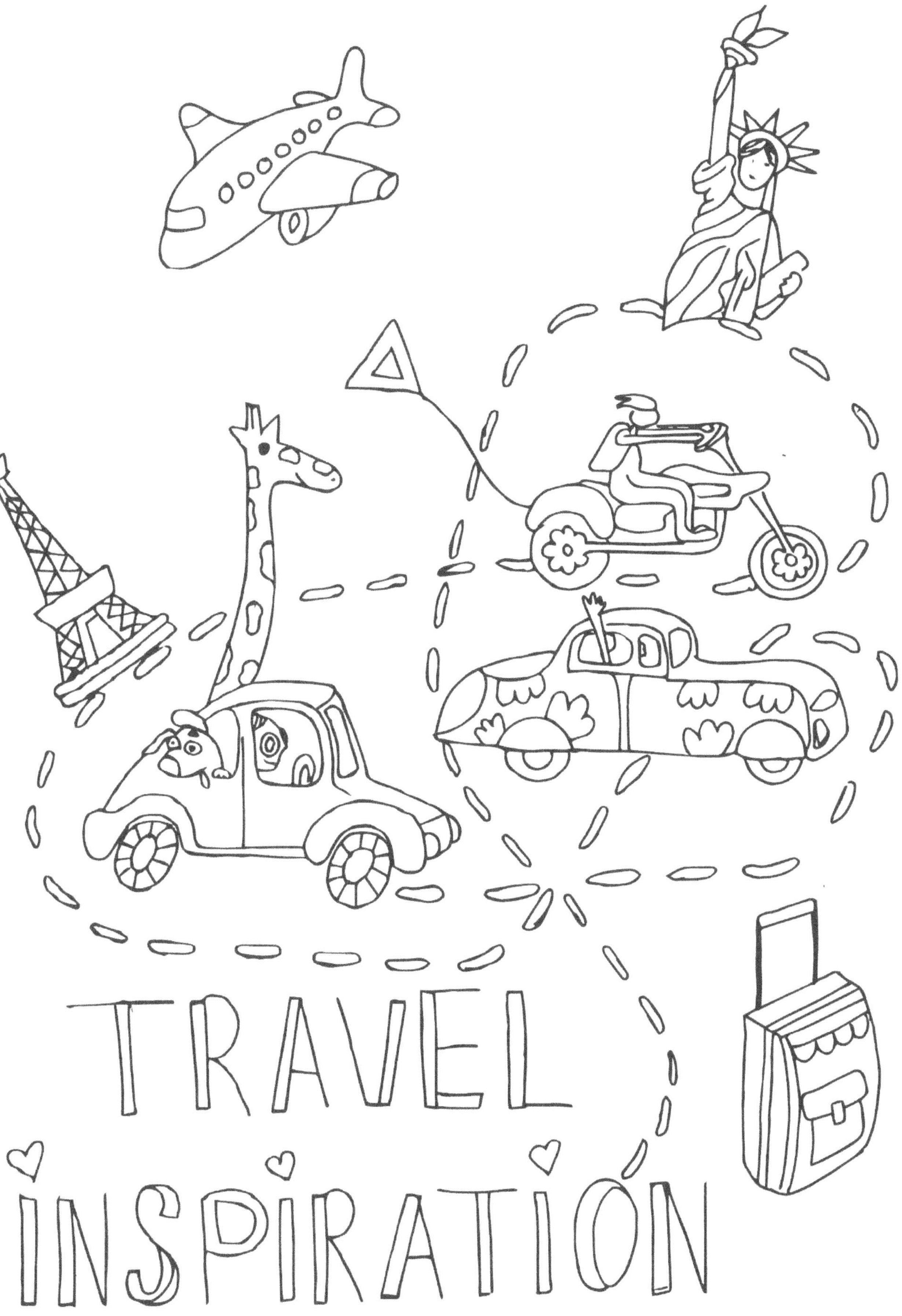
TRAVEL
INSPIRATION

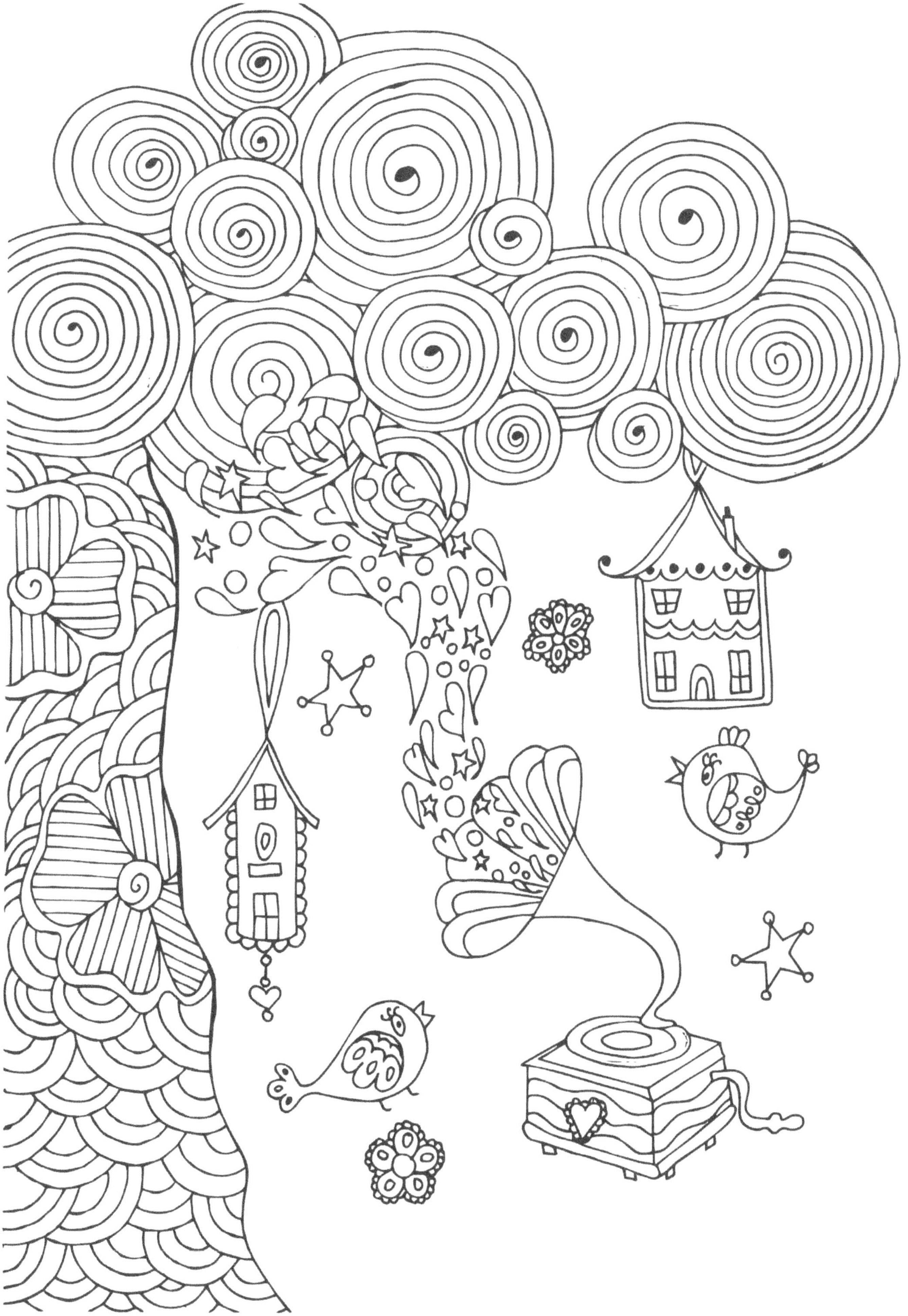

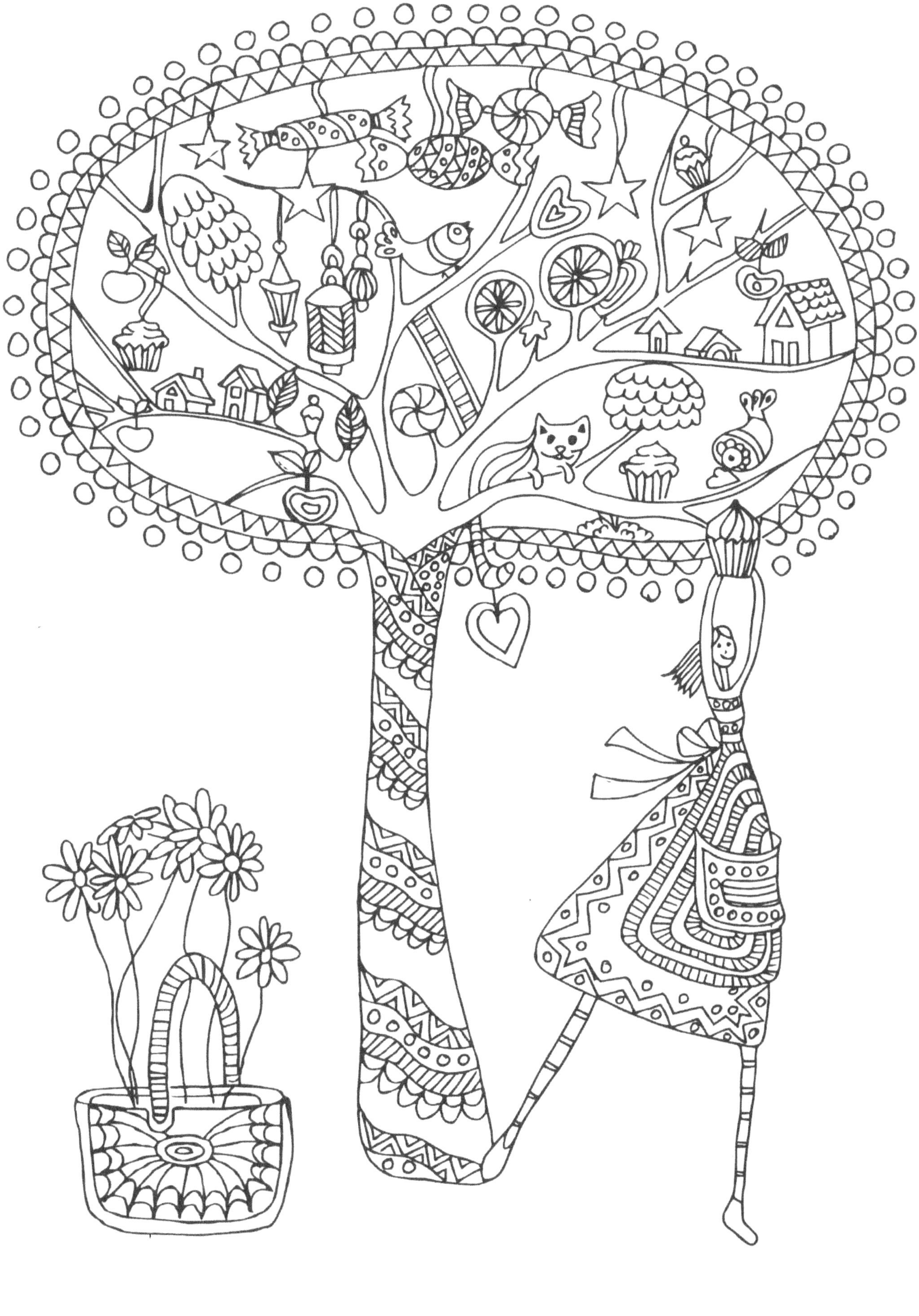

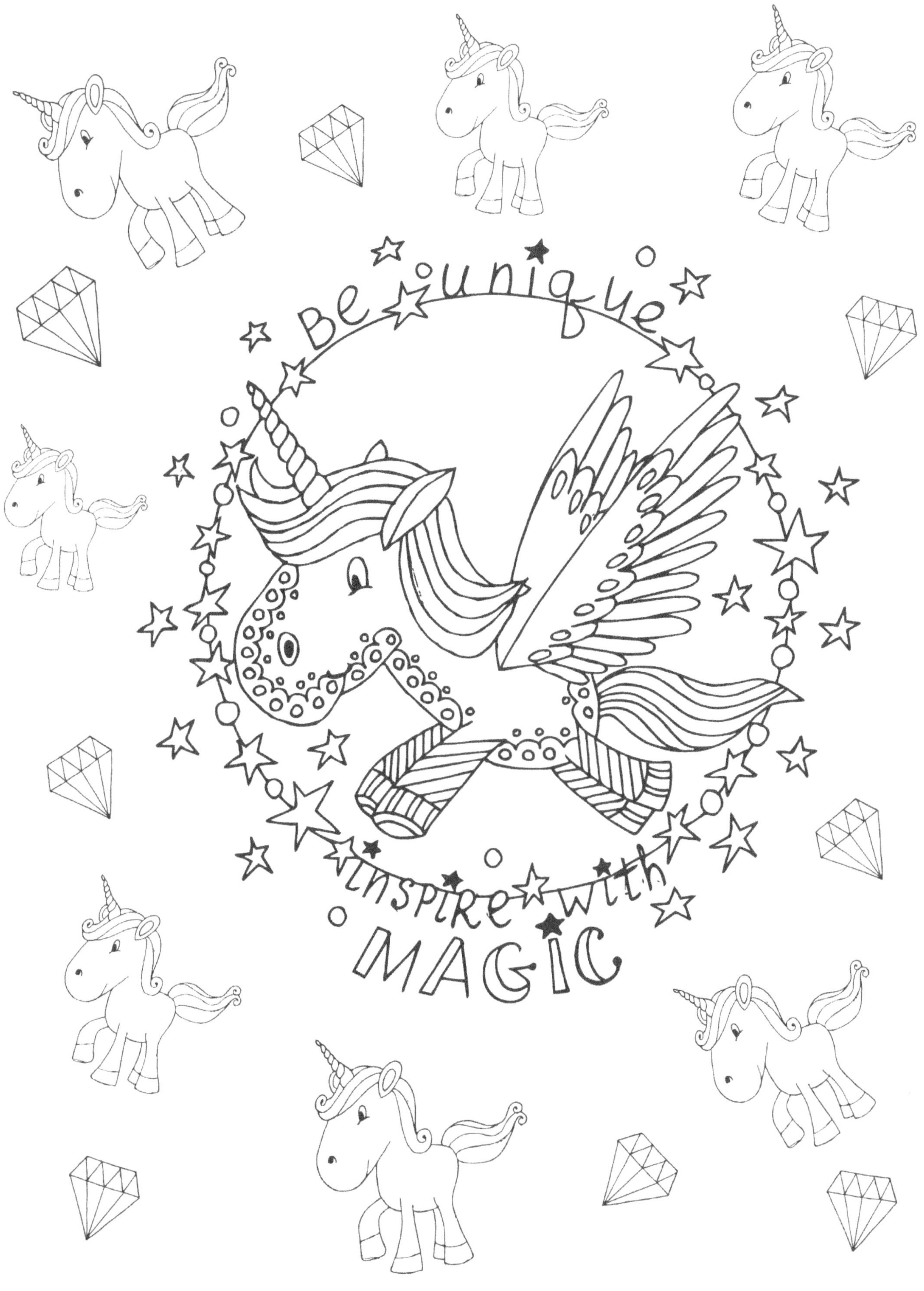
Be unique
inspire with
MAGIC

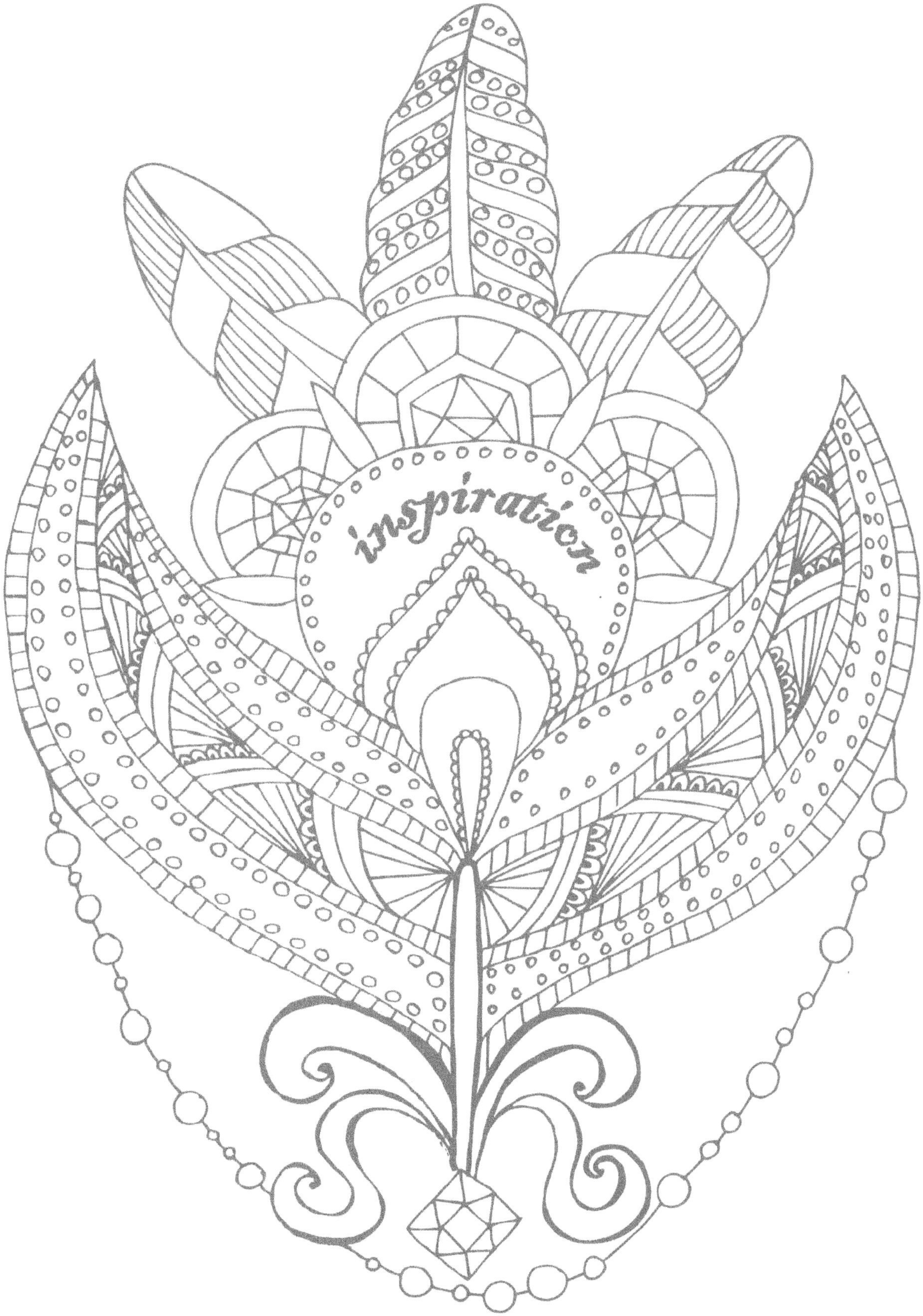
inspiration

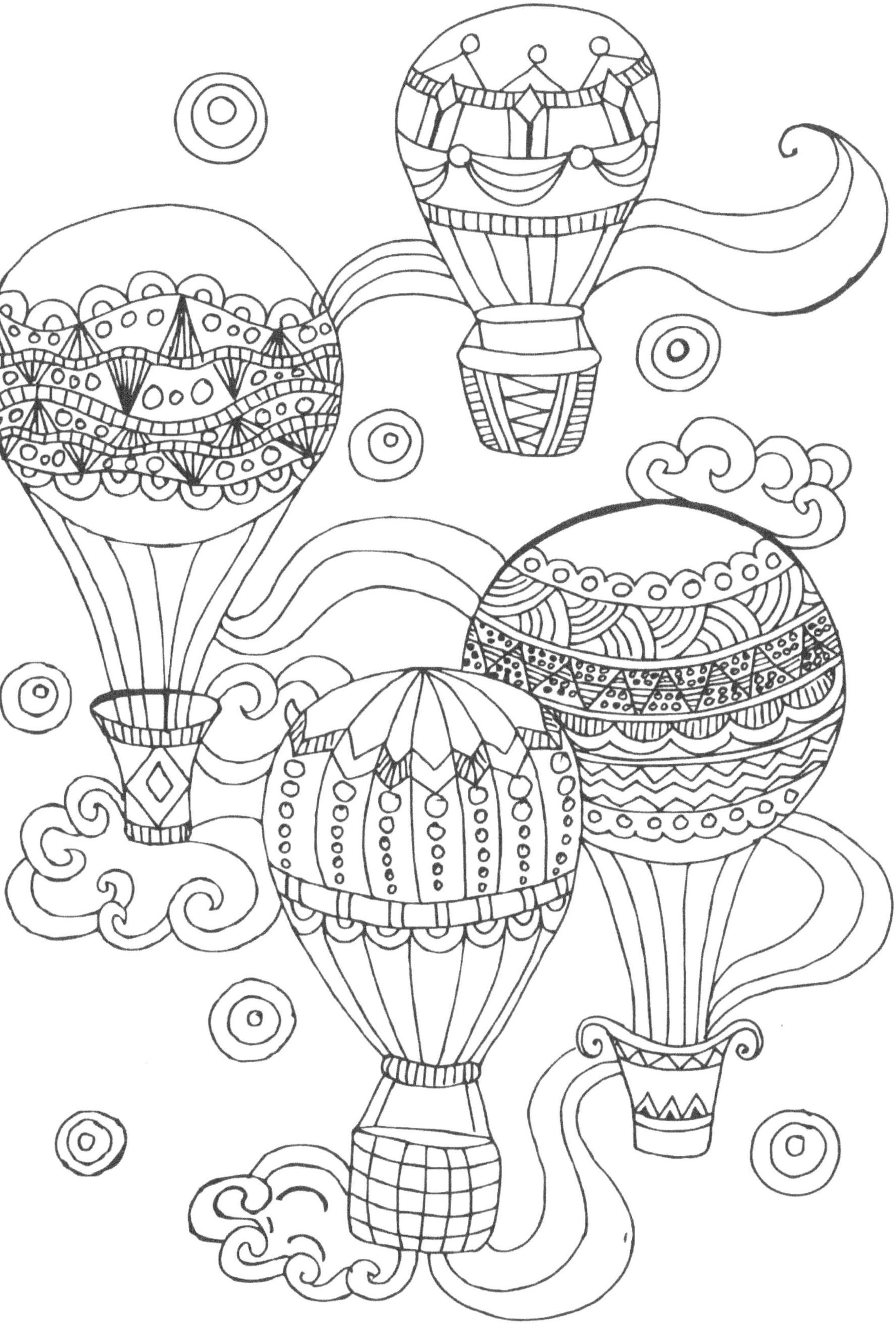

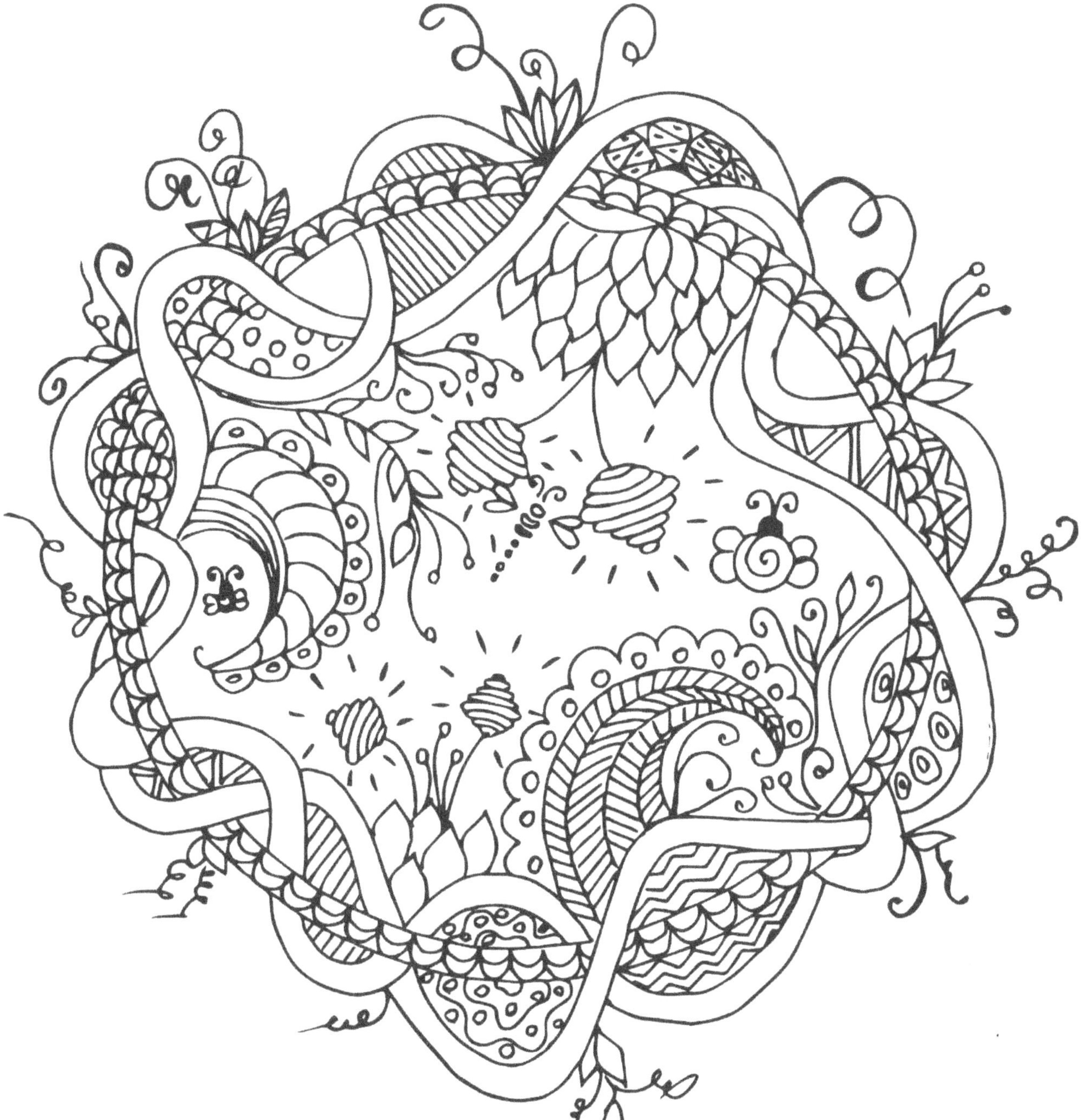

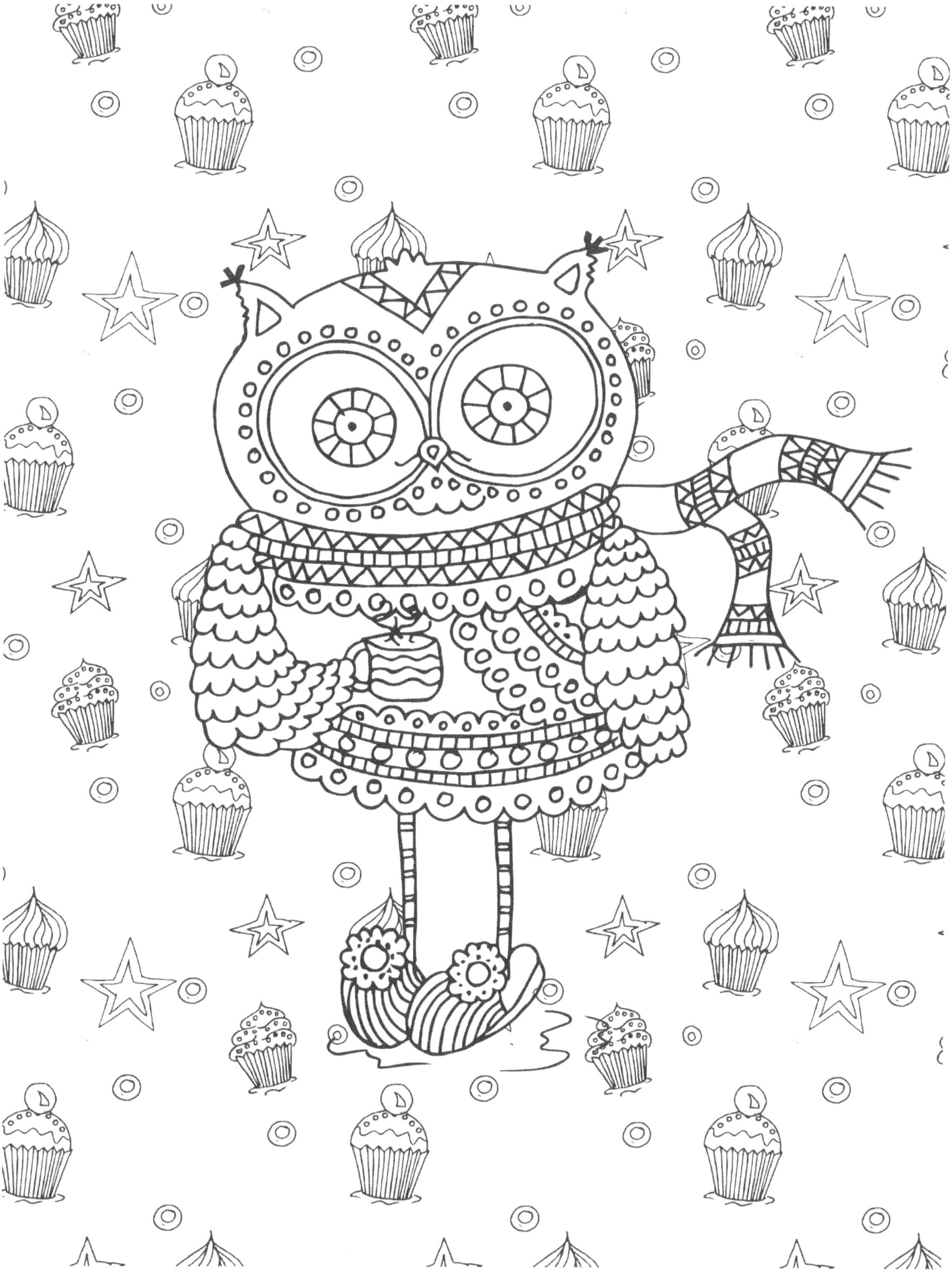

www.ingramcontent.com/pod-product-compliance
Lightning Source LLC
Chambersburg PA
CBHW081210180526
45170CB00006B/2282
*9781523283743*